W9-ABI-388

Modern Critical Interpretations

Thomas Hardy's

The Return of the Native

Modern Critical Interpretations

The Oresteia
Beowulf
The General Prologue to The Canterbury Tales
The Pardoner's Tale
The Knight's Tale
The Divine Comedy
Exodus
Genesis
The Gospels
The Iliad
The Book of Job
Volpone
Doctor Faustus
The Revelation of St. John the Divine
The Song of Songs
Oedipus Rex
The Aeneid
The Duchess of Malfi
Antony and Cleopatra
As You Like It
Coriolanus
Hamlet
Henry IV, Part I
Henry IV, Part II
Henry V
Julius Caesar
King Lear
Macbeth
Measure for Measure
The Merchant of Venice
A Midsummer Night's Dream
Much Ado About Nothing
Othello
Richard II
Richard III
The Sonnets
Taming of the Shrew
The Tempest
Twelfth Night
The Winter's Tale
Emma
Mansfield Park
Pride and Prejudice
The Life of Samuel Johnson
Moll Flanders
Robinson Crusoe
Tom Jones
The Beggar's Opera
Gray's Elegy
Paradise Lost
The Rape of the Lock
Tristram Shandy
Gulliver's Travels
Evelina
The Marriage of Heaven and Hell
Songs of Innocence and Experience
Jane Eyre
Wuthering Heights
Don Juan
The Rime of the Ancient Mariner
Bleak House
David Copperfield
Hard Times
A Tale of Two Cities
Middlemarch
The Mill on the Floss
Jude the Obscure
The Mayor of Casterbridge
The Return of the Native
Tess of the D'Urbervilles
The Odes of Keats
Frankenstein
Vanity Fair
Barchester Towers
The Prelude
The Red Badge of Courage
The Scarlet Letter
The Ambassadors
Daisy Miller, The Turn of the Screw, and Other Tales
The Portrait of a Lady
Billy Budd, Benito Cereno, Bartleby the Scrivener, and Other Tales
Moby-Dick
The Tales of Poe
Walden
Adventures of Huckleberry Finn
The Life of Frederick Douglass
Heart of Darkness
Lord Jim
Nostromo
A Passage to India
Dubliners
A Portrait of the Artist as a Young Man
Ulysses
Kim
The Rainbow
Sons and Lovers
Women in Love
1984
Major Barbara
Man and Superman
Pygmalion
St. Joan
The Playboy of the Western World
The Importance of Being Earnest
Mrs. Dalloway
To the Lighthouse
My Antonia
An American Tragedy
Murder in the Cathedral
The Waste Land
Absalom, Absalom!
Light in August
Sanctuary
The Sound and the Fury
The Great Gatsby
A Farewell to Arms
The Sun Also Rises
Arrowsmith
Lolita
The Iceman Cometh
Long Day's Journey Into Night
The Grapes of Wrath
Miss Lonelyhearts
The Glass Menagerie
A Streetcar Named Desire
Their Eyes Were Watching God
Native Son
Waiting for Godot
Herzog
All My Sons
Death of a Salesman
Gravity's Rainbow
All the King's Men
The Left Hand of Darkness
The Brothers Karamazov
Crime and Punishment
Madame Bovary
The Interpretation of Dreams
The Castle
The Metamorphosis
The Trial
Man's Fate
The Magic Mountain
Montaigne's Essays
Remembrance of Things Past
The Red and the Black
Anna Karenina
War and Peace

These and other titles in preparation

Modern Critical Interpretations

Thomas Hardy's
The Return of the Native

Edited and with an introduction by

Harold Bloom

Sterling Professor of the Humanities

Yale University

Chelsea House Publishers

NEW YORK ◇ PHILADELPHIA

Printed and bound in the United States of America

10 9 8 7 6 5 4 3 2

∞ The paper used in this publication meets the minimum requirements of the American National Standard for Permanence of Paper for Printed Library Materials, Z39.48-1984.

Library of Congress Cataloging-in-Publication Data
Thomas Hardy's The return of the native.
(Modern critical interpretations)
Bibliography: p.
Includes index.
Summary: A collection of eight critical essays on Hardy's novel "The Return of the Native" arranged in chronological order of publication.
1. Hardy, Thomas, 1840–1928. Return of the native.
[1. Hardy, Thomas, 1840–1928. Return of the native.
2. English literature—History and criticism] I. Bloom, Harold.
PR4747.B55 1987 823′.8 87-11795
ISBN 0-87754-743-2

Contents

Editor's Note

This book gathers together a representative selection of the best modern interpretations of Thomas Hardy's novel *The Return of the Native*. The critical essays are reprinted here in the chronological order of their original publication. I am grateful to David Parker for his work as a researcher upon this volume.

My introduction first considers the relation of Hardy to Schopenhauer and to Shelley and then centers upon both Eustacia and Egdon Heath, so as to characterize the novel's most vital character and its disturbing context.

D. H. Lawrence, Hardy's true heir as a novelist, begins the chronological sequence with a meditation upon Clym's failure to be a true match for Eustacia. Clearly seeing the *Return*'s faults, Irving Howe nevertheless praises the novel for Hardy's representation of human pain.

In the reading of Jean R. Brooks, the *Return* is seen as "concerned with the Promethean struggle of conscious life against the unconscious 'rayless' universe from which it sprang."

Eustacia Vye is the subject of David Eggenschwiler's exegesis, which sees her as the consequence of a dialectical struggle in Hardy with regard to his own Romanticism. That struggle is analyzed in Freudian terms by Perry Meisel, for whom Eustacia and her story represent Hardy's own return of the repressed.

Ian Gregor salutes the *Return* as Hardy's first major novel, basing this judgment on the importance of Hardy's portrait of an authentic contemporary consciousness in Clym. In Avrom Fleishman's reading, Egdon Heath figures both as person and as metaphor.

Bruce Johnson concludes this book with praise for the *Return* as a "modern pastoral," Hardy's rejuvenation of the ancient genre, a revisionary act that combines tragedy and pastoral in the character of Clym, who participates as protagonist in both modes.

Introduction

I

For Arthur Schopenhauer, the Will to Live was the true thing-in-itself, not an interpretation but a rapacious, active, universal, and ultimately indifferent drive or desire. Schopenhauer's great work, *The World as Will and Representation,* had the same relation to and influence upon many of the principal nineteenth- and early twentieth-century novelists that Freud's writings have in regard to many of this century's later, crucial masters of prose fiction. Zola, Maupassant, Turgenev, and Tolstoy join Thomas Hardy as Schopenhauer's nineteenth-century heirs, in a tradition that goes on through Proust, Conrad, and Thomas Mann to culminate in aspects of Borges, and of Beckett, the most eminent living writer of narrative. Since Schopenhauer (despite Freud's denials) was one of Freud's prime precursors, one could argue that aspects of Freud's influence upon writers simply carry on from Schopenhauer's previous effect. Manifestly, the relation of Schopenhauer to Hardy is different both in kind and degree from the larger sense in which Schopenhauer was Freud's forerunner or Wittgenstein's. A poet-novelist like Hardy turns to a rhetorical speculator like Schopenhauer only because he finds something in his own temperament and sensibility confirmed and strengthened, and not at all as Lucretius turned to Epicurus, or as Whitman was inspired by Emerson.

The true precursor for Hardy was Shelley, whose visionary skepticism permeates the novels as well as the poems and *The Dynasts*. There is some technical debt to George Eliot in the early novels, but Hardy in his depths was little more moved by her than by Wilkie Collins, from whom he also learned elements of craft. Shelley's tragic sense of eros is pervasive throughout Hardy, and ultimately determines Hardy's understanding of his strongest heroines: Bathsheba Everdene, Eustacia Vye, Marty South, Tess Durbeyfield, Sue Bridehead. Between desire and fulfillment in Shelley falls the shadow of the selfhood, a shadow that makes love and what might be called the means of love quite irreconcilable. What M. D. Zabel named as "the aesthetic of incongruity" in Hardy and ascribed to temperamental causes is in a profound way the result of attempting to transmute the procedures of *The Revolt of Islam* and *Epipsychidion* into the supposedly naturalistic novel.

J. Hillis Miller, when he worked more in the mode of a critic of consciousness like Georges Poulet than in the deconstruction of Paul de Man and Jacques Derrida, saw the fate of love in Hardy as being darkened always by a shadow cast by the lover's consciousness itself. Hugh Kenner, with a distaste for Hardy akin to (and perhaps derived from) T. S. Eliot's in *After Strange Gods,* suggested that Miller had created a kind of Proustian Hardy, who turns out to be a case rather than an artist. Hardy was certainly not an artist comparable to Henry James (who dismissed him as a mere imitator of George Eliot) or James Joyce, but the High Modernist shibboleths for testing the novel have now waned considerably, except in a few surviving high priests of Modernism like Kenner. A better guide to Hardy's permanent strength as a novelist was his heir D. H. Lawrence, whose *The Rainbow* and *Women in Love* marvelously brought Hardy's legacy to an apotheosis. Lawrence, praising Hardy with a rebel son's ambivalence, associated him with Tolstoy as a tragic writer:

> And this is the quality Hardy shares with the great writers, Shakespeare or Sophocles or Tolstoi, this setting behind the small action of his protagonists the terrific action of unfathomed nature; setting a smaller system of morality, the one grasped and formulated by the human consciousness within the vast, uncomprehended and incomprehensible morality of nature or of life itself, surpassing human consciousness. The difference is, that whereas in Shakespeare or Sophocles the greater, uncomprehended morality, or fate, is actively transgressed and gives active punishment, in Hardy and Tolstoi the lesser, human morality, the mechanical system is actively transgressed, and holds, and punishes the protagonist, whilst the greater morality is only passively, negatively transgressed, it is represented merely as being present in background, in scenery, not taking any active part, having no direct connexion with the protagonist. (OEdipus, Hamlet, Macbeth set themselves up against, or find themselves set up against, the unfathomed moral forces of nature, and out of this unfathomed force comes their death. Whereas

> enina, Eustacia, Tess, Sue, and Jude find themselves up against the established system of human government and morality, they cannot detach themselves, and are brought down. Their real tragedy is that they are unfaithful to the greater unwritten morality, which would have bidden Anna Karenina be patient and wait until she, by virtue of greater right, could take what she needed from society; would have bidden Vronsky detach himself from the system, become an individual, creating a new colony of morality with Anna; would have bidden Eustacia fight Clym for his own soul, and Tess take and claim her Angel, since she had the greater light; would have bidden Jude and Sue endure for very honour's sake, since one must bide by the best that one has known, and not succumb to the lesser good.
>
> ("Study of Thomas Hardy")

This seems to me powerful and just, because it catches what is most surprising and enduring in Hardy's novels—the sublime stature and aesthetic dignity of his crucial protagonists—while exposing also his great limitation, his denial of freedom to his best personages. Lawrence's prescription for what would have saved Eustacia and Clym, Tess and Angel, Sue and Jude, is perhaps not as persuasive. He speaks of them as though they were Gudrun and Gerald, and thus have failed to be Ursula and Birkin. It is Hardy's genius that they are what they had to be: as imperfect as their creator and his vision, as impure as his language and his plotting, and finally painful and memorable to us:

> Note that, in this bitterness, delight,
> Since the imperfect is so hot in us,
> Lies in flawed words and stubborn sounds.

II

I first read *The Return of the Native* when I was about fifteen, forty years ago, and had reread it in whole or in part several times through the years before rereading it now. What I had remembered most vividly then I am likely to remember again: Eustacia, Venn the red man, the Heath. I had almost forgotten Clym, and his mother, and Thomasin, and Wildeve, and probably will forget them again. Clym, in particular, is a weak failure in characterization, and nearly sinks the novel; indeed ought to capsize any novel whatsoever. Yet *The Return of the Native* survives him, even though its chief glory, the sexually enchanting Eustacia Vye, does not. Her suicide is so much the waste of a marvelous woman (or representation of a woman, if you insist upon being a formalist) that the reader finds Clym even more intolerable than he is, and is likely not to forgive Hardy, except that Hardy clearly suffers the loss quite as much as any reader does.

Eustacia underwent a singular transformation during the novel's composition, from a daemonic sort of female Byron, or Byronic witch-like creature, to the grandly beautiful, discontented, and human—all too human but hardly blameworthy—heroine, who may be the most desirable woman in all of nineteenth-century British fiction. "A powerful personality uncurbed by any institutional attachment or by submission to any objective beliefs; unhampered by any ideas"—it would be a good description of Eustacia, but is actually Hardy himself through the eyes of T. S. Eliot in *After Strange Gods,* where Hardy is chastised for not believing in Original Sin and deplored also because "at times his style touches sublimity without ever having passed through the stage of being good."

Here is Eustacia in the early "Queen of Night" chapter:

> She was in person full-limbed and somewhat heavy; without ruddiness, as without pallor; and soft to the touch as a cloud. To see her hair was to fancy that a whole winter did not contain darkness enough to form its shadow: it closed over her forehead like nightfall extinguishing the western glow.
>
> Her nerves extended into those tresses, and her temper could always be softened by stroking them down. When her hair was brushed she would instantly sink into stillness and look like the Sphinx. If, in passing under one of the Egdon banks, any of its thick skeins were caught, as they sometimes were, by a prickly tuft of the large *Ulex Europaeus*—which will act as a sort of hairbrush—she would go back a few steps, and pass against it a second time.
>
> She had Pagan eyes, full of nocturnal mysteries, and their light, as it came and went, and came again, was partially hampered by their oppressive lids and lashes; and of these the under lid was much fuller than it usually is with English women. This enabled her to indulge in reverie without seeming to do so: she might have been believed capable of sleeping without closing them up. Assuming that the souls of men and women were visible essences, you could fancy the colour of Eustacia's soul to be flame-like. The sparks from it that rose into her dark pupils gave the same impression.

Hardy's Eustacia may owe something to Walter Pater's *The Renaissance,* published five years before *The Return of the Native,* since in some ways she makes a third with Pater's evocations of the Botticelli Venus and Leonardo's Mona Lisa, visions of antithetical female sexuality. Eustacia's flame-like quality precisely recalls Pater's ecstasy of passion in the "Conclusion" to *The Renaissance,* and the epigraph to *The Return of the Native* could well have been:

> This at least of flame-like our life has, that it is but the concurrence, renewed from moment to moment, of forces parting sooner or later on their ways.

This at least of flame-like Eustacia's life has, that the concurrence of forces parts sooner rather than later. But then this most beautiful of Hardy's women is also the most doom-eager, the color of her soul being flame-like. The Heath brings her only Wildeve and Clym, but Paris doubtless would have brought her scarce better, since as Queen of Night she attracts the constancy and the kindness of sorrow.

If Clym and Wildeve are bad actors, and they are, what about Egdon Heath? On this, critics are perpetually divided, some finding the landscape sublime, while others protest that its representation is bathetic. I myself am divided, since clearly it is both, and sometimes simultaneously so! Though Eustacia hates it fiercely, it is nearly as Shelleyan as she is, and rather less natural than presumably it ought to be. That it is more overwritten than overgrown is palpable:

> To recline on a stump of thorn in the central valley of Egdon, between afternoon and night, as now, where the eye could reach nothing of the world outside the summits and shoulders of heathland which filled the whole circumference of its glance, and to know that everything around and underneath had been from prehistoric times as unaltered as the stars overhead, gave ballast to the mind adrift on change, and harassed by the irrepressible New. The great inviolate place had an ancient permanence which the sea cannot claim. Who can say of a particular sea that it is old? Distilled by the sun, kneaded by the moon, it is renewed in a year, in a day, or in an hour. The sea changed, the fields changed, the rivers, the villages, and the people changed, yet Egdon remained. Those surfaces were neither so steep as to be destructible by weather, nor so flat as to be the victims of floods and deposits. With the exception of an aged highway, and a still more aged barrow presently to be referred to—themselves al-

> most crystallized to natural products by long continuance—even the trifling irregularities were not caused by pickaxe, plough, or spade, but remained as the very finger-touches of the last geological change.

Even Melville cannot always handle this heightened mode; Hardy rarely can, although he attempts it often. And yet we do remember Egdon Heath, years after reading the novel, possibly because something about it wounds us even as it wounds Eustacia. We remember also Diggory Venn, not as the prosperous burgher he becomes, but as we first encounter him, permeated by the red ochre of his picturesque trade:

> The decayed officer, by degrees, came up alongside his fellow-wayfarer, and wished him good evening. The reddleman turned his head and replied in sad and occupied tones. He was young, and his face, if not exactly handsome, approached so near to handsome that nobody would have contradicted an assertion that it really was so in its natural colour. His eye, which glared so strangely through his stain, was in itself attractive—keen as that of a bird of prey, and blue as autumn mist. He had neither whisker nor moustache, which allowed the soft curves of the lower part of his face to be apparent. His lips were thin, and though, as it seemed, compressed by thought, there was a pleasant twitch at their corners now and then. He was clothed throughout in a tight-fitting suit of corduroy, excellent in quality, not much worn, and well-chosen for its purpose; but deprived of its original colour by his trade. It showed to advantage the good shape of his figure. A certain well-to-do air about the man suggested that he was not poor for his degree. The natural query of an observer would have been, Why should such a promising being as this have hidden his prepossessing exterior by adopting that singular occupation?

Hardy had intended Venn to disappear mysteriously forever from Egdon Heath, instead of marrying Thomasin, but yielded to the anxiety of giving the contemporary reader something cheerful and normative at the end of his austere and dark novel. He ought to have kept to his intent, but perhaps it does not matter. The Heath endures, the red man either vanishes or is transmogrified into a husband and a burgher. Though we see Clym rather uselessly preaching to all comers as the book closes, our spirits are elsewhere, with the wild image of longing that no longer haunts the Heath, Hardy's lost Queen of Night.

From "Study of Thomas Hardy": *The Return of the Native*

D. H. Lawrence

[*The Return of the Native*] is the first tragic and important novel. Eustacia, dark, wild, passionate, quite conscious of her desires and inheriting no tradition which would make her ashamed of them, since she is of a novelistic Italian birth, loves, first, the unstable Wildeve, who does not satisfy her, then casts him aside for the newly returned Clym, whom she marries. What does she want? She does not know, but it is evidently some form of self-realization; she wants to be herself, to attain herself. But she does not know how, by what means, so romantic imagination says, Paris and the beau monde. As if that would have stayed her unsatisfaction.

Clym has found out the vanity of Paris and the beau monde. What, then, does he want? He does not know; his imagination tells him he wants to serve the moral system of the community, since the material system is despicable. He wants to teach little Egdon boys in school. There is as much vanity in this, easily, as in Eustacia's Paris. For what is the moral system but the ratified form of the material system? What is Clym's altruism but a deep, very subtle cowardice, that makes him shirk his own being whilst apparently acting nobly; which makes him choose to improve mankind rather than to struggle at the quick of himself into being. He is not able to undertake his own soul, so he will take a commission for society to enlighten the souls of others. It is a subtle equivocation. Thus both Eustacia and he sidetrack from themselves, and each leaves the other unconvinced, unsat-

---

From *Phoenix: The Posthumous Papers of D. H. Lawrence*, edited by Edward D. McDonald. Viking, 1936.

isfied, unrealized. Eustacia, because she moves outside the convention, must die; Clym, because he identified himself with the community, is transferred from Paris to preaching. He had never become an integral man, because when faced with the demand to produce himself, he remained under cover of the community and excused by his altruism.

His remorse over his mother is adulterated with sentiment; it is exaggerated by the push of tradition behind it. Even in this he does not ring true. He is always according to pattern, producing his feelings more or less on demand, according to the accepted standard. Practically never is he able to act or even feel in his original self; he is always according to the convention. His punishment is his final loss of all his original self: he is left preaching, out of sheer emptiness.

Thomasin and Venn have nothing in them turbulent enough to push them to the bounds of the convention. There is always room for them inside. They are genuine people, and they get the prize within the walls.

Wildeve, shifty and unhappy, attracted always from outside and never driven from within, can neither stand with nor without the established system. He cares nothing for it, because he is unstable, has no positive being. He is an eternal assumption.

The other victim, Clym's mother, is the crashing-down of one of the old, rigid pillars of the system. The pressure on her is too great. She is weakened from the inside also, for her nature is nonconventional; it cannot own the bounds.

So, in this book, all the exceptional people, those with strong feelings and unusual characters, are reduced; only those remain who are steady and genuine, if commonplace. Let a man will for himself, and he is destroyed. He must will according to the established system.

The real sense of tragedy is got from the setting. What is the great, tragic power in the book? It is Egdon Heath. And who are the real spirits of the Heath? First, Eustacia, then Clym's mother, then Wildeve. The natives have little or nothing in common with the place.

What is the real stuff of tragedy in the book? It is the Heath. It is the primitive, primal earth, where the instinctive life heaves up. There, in the deep, rude stirring of the instincts, there was the reality that worked the tragedy. Close to the body of things, there can be heard the stir that makes us and destroys us. The heath heaved with raw instinct. Egdon, whose dark soil was strong and crude and organic as the body of a beast. Out of the body of this crude earth are born Eustacia, Wildeve, Mistress Yeobright, Clym, and all the others. They are one year's accidental crop. What matters if some are drowned or dead, and others preaching or married: what matter, any more than the withering heath, the reddening berries, the seedy furze, and the dead fern of one autumn of Egdon? The Heath persists. Its body is strong and fecund, it will bear many more crops beside this. Here is the sombre, latent power that will go on producing no matter what happens to the product. Here is the deep, black source from whence all these little contents of lives are drawn. And the contents of the small lives are spilled and wasted. There is savage satisfaction in it: for so much more remains to come, such a black, powerful fecundity is working there that what does it matter?

Three people die and are taken back into the Heath; they mingle their strong earth again with its powerful soil, having been broken off at their stem. It is very good. Not Egdon is futile, sending forth life on the powerful heave of passion. It cannot be futile, for it is eternal. What is futile is the purpose of man.

Man has a purpose which he has divorced from the passionate purpose that issued him out of the earth into being. The Heath threw forth its shaggy heather and furze and fern, clean into being. It threw forth Eustacia and Wildeve and Mistress Yeobright and Clym, but to what purpose? Eustacia thought she wanted the hats and bonnets of Paris. Perhaps she was right. The heavy, strong soil of Egdon, breeding original native beings, is under Paris as well as under Wessex, and Eustacia sought herself in the gay city. She thought life there, in Paris, would be tropical, and all her energy and passion out of Egdon would there come into handsome flower. And if Paris real had been Paris as she imagined it, no doubt she was right, and her instinct was soundly expressed. But Paris real was not Eustacia's imagined Paris. Where was her imagined Paris, the place where her powerful nature could come to blossom? Beside some strong-passioned, unconfined man, her mate.

Which mate Clym might have been. He was born out of passionate Egdon to live as a passionate being whose strong feelings moved him ever further into being. But quite early his life became narrowed down to a small purpose: he must of necessity go into business, and submit his whole being, body and soul as well as mind, to the business and to the greater system it represented. His feelings, that should have produced the man, were suppressed and contained, he worked according to a system imposed from without. The dark struggle of Egdon, a struggle into being as the furze struggles into flower, went on in him, but could not burst the enclosure of the idea, the system which contained him. Impotent to *be,* he must transform himself, and live in an abstraction, in a generalization, he must identify himself with the system. He must live as Man or Humanity, or as the Community, or as Society, or as Civilization. "An inner strenuousness was preying on his outer symmetry, and they rated his look as singular. . . . His countenance was overlaid with legible meanings. Without being thought-worn, he yet had certain marks derived from a perception of his surroundings, such as are not infrequently found on man at the end of the four or five years of endeavour which follow the close of placid pupilage. He already showed that thought is a disease of the flesh, and indirectly bore evidence that ideal physical beauty is incompatible with emotional development and a full recognition of the coil of things. Mental luminousness must be fed with the oil of life, even if there is already a physical seed for it; and the pitiful sight of two demands on one supply was just showing itself here."

But did the face of Clym show that thought is a disease of flesh, or merely that in this case a dis-ease, an un-ease, of flesh produced thought? One does not catch thought like a fever: one produces it. If it be in any way a disease of flesh, it is rather the rash that indicates the disease than the disease itself. The "inner strenuousness" of Clym's nature was not fighting against his physical symmetry, but against the limits imposed on his physical movement. By nature, as a passionate, violent product of Egdon, he should have loved and suffered in flesh and in soul from love, long before this age. He should have lived and moved and had his being, whereas he had only his business, and afterwards his inactivity. His years of pupilage were past, "he was one of whom something original was expected," yet he continued in pupilage. For he produced nothing original in being or in act, and certainly no original thought. None of his ideas were original. Even he himself was not original. He was over-taught, and become an echo. His life had been arrested, and his activity turned into repetition. Far from being emotionally developed, he was emotionally undeveloped, almost entirely. Only his mental faculties were developed. And, hid, his emotions were obliged to work according to the label he put upon them: a ready-made label.

Yet he remained for all that an original, the force of life was in him, however much he frustrated and suppressed its natural movement. "As is usual with bright natures, the deity that lies ignominiously chained within an ephemeral human carcass shone out of him like a ray." But was the deity chained within his ephemeral human carcass, or within his limited human consciousness? Was it his blood, which rose dark and potent out of Egdon, which hampered and confined the deity, or was it his mind, that house built of extraneous knowledge and guarded by his will, which formed the prison?

He came back to Egdon—what for? To reunite himself with the strong, free flow of life that rose out of Egdon as from a source? No—"to preach to the Egdon eremites that they might rise to a serene comprehensiveness without going through the process of enriching themselves." As if the Egdon eremites had not already far more serene comprehensiveness than ever he had himself, rooted as they were in the soil of all things, and living from the root! What did it matter how they enriched themselves, so long as they kept this strong, deep root in the primal soil, so long as their instincts moved out to action and to expression? The system was big enough for them, and had no power over their instincts. They should have taught him rather than he them.

And Egdon made him marry Eustacia. Here was action and life, here was a move into being on his part. But as soon as he got her, she became an idea to him, she had to fit in his system of ideas. According to his way of living, he knew her already, she was labelled and classed and fixed down. He had got into this way of living, and he could not get out of it. He had identified himself with the system, and he could not extricate himself. He did not know that Eustacia had her being beyond his. He did not know that she existed untouched by his system and his mind, where no system had sway and where no consciousness had risen to the surface. He did not know that she was Egdon, the powerful, eternal origin seething with production. He thought he knew. Egdon to him was the tract of common land, producing familiar rough herbage, and having some few unenlightened inhabitants. So he skated over heaven and hell, and having made a map of the surface, thought he knew all. But underneath and among his mapped world, the eternal powerful fecundity worked on heedless of him and his arrogance. His preaching, his superficiality made no difference. What did it matter if he had calculated a moral chart from the surface of life? Could that affect life, any more than a chart of the heavens affects the stars, affects the whole stellar universe which exists beyond our knowledge? Could the sound of his words affect the working of the body of Egdon, where in the unfathomable womb was begot and conceived all that would ever come forth? Did not his own heart beat far removed and immune from his thinking and talking? Had he been able to put even his own heart's mysterious resonance upon his map, from which he charted the course of lives in his moral system? And how much more completely, then, had he left out, in utter ignorance, the dark, powerful source whence all things rise into being, whence they will always continue to rise, to struggle forward to further being? A little of the static surface he could see, and map out. Then he thought his map was the thing itself. How blind he was, how utterly blind to the tremendous movement carrying and producing the surface. He did not know that the greater part of every life is underground, like roots in the dark in contact with the beyond. He preached, thinking lives could be moved like hen-houses from here to there. His blindness indeed brought on the calamity. But what matter if Eustacia or Wildeve or Mrs. Yeobright died: what matter if he himself became a mere rattle of repetitive words—what did it matter? It was regrettable; no more. Egdon, the primal impulsive body, would go on producing all that was to be produced, eternally, though the will of man should destroy the blossom yet in bud, over and over again. At last he must learn what it is to be at one, in his mind and will, with the primal impulses that rise in him. Till then, let him perish or preach. The great reality on which the little tragedies enact themselves cannot be detracted from. The will and words which militate against it are the only vanity.

This is a constant revelation in Hardy's novels: that there exists a great background, vital and vivid, which matters more than the people who move upon it. Against the background of dark, passionate Egdon, of the leafy, sappy passion and sentiment of the woodlands, of the unfathomed stars, is drawn the lesser scheme of lives: *The Return of the Native, The Woodlanders,* or *Two on a Tower.* Upon the vast, incomprehensible pattern of some primal morality greater than ever the human mind can grasp, is drawn the little, pathetic pattern of man's moral life and struggle, pathetic, almost ridiculous. The little fold of law and order, the little walled city within which man has to defend himself from the waste enormity of nature, becomes always too small, and the pioneers venturing out with the code of the walled city upon them, die in the bonds of that code, free and yet unfree, preaching the walled city and looking to the waste.

The Return of the Native

Irving Howe

The Return of the Native is the first book in which Hardy reaches toward grandiose "literary" effects and announces those grim preoccupations with fatality that will become associated with his name. Though he continues to serve as chronicler of Wessex and to employ, with a new and more artful self-consciousness, his repertoire of folk motifs, Hardy now brings to bear upon this little world an array of intellectual and historical pressures that were not to be seen in his earlier books. The fixed country setting is shaken by voices of discontent, the bonds of social solidarity begin to loosen, the characters are overcome by feelings of boredom and estrangement, and a new kind of sexuality, neurotically willful but also perversely enticing, makes its appearance. A thick cloud—the cloud of a modern inherently problematic consciousness—falls across the horizon of Wessex, and neither virtue nor prayer, will nor magic can remove it.

In almost every critical study of Hardy's work written before the Second World War, as in almost every history of the English novel, the accepted valuation of *The Return of the Native* is that here, beyond doubt, is his first major novel. Decorated with imprecisions about the symbolic resonance of Egdon Heath and the philosophic depths of Hardy's pessimism, this is a judgment now hard to accept. It is hard to accept because the book so clearly falls short of classical rank or resolution, so clearly is a work of stammering awkwardness, unused possibilities and naive bravura. Yet the book does survive, not merely as a classroom favorite enabling one's entry into the adult world, but also as a work that, reread in later years, can still seem impressive in a strange and gaunt way.

Nineteenth-century England has given us a number of such books (*Silas Marner, David Copperfield*) which yield pleasure and reach toward buried pockets of emotion, yet cannot quite be regarded as mature works of art in the way that *Middlemarch* or *Nostromo* or *The Bostonians* can. We may try to get round this problem by calling novels like *Silas Marner* and *The Return of the Native* "popular classics," but this is merely to provide a label where analysis is wanted. Such works—it can at least be noted—present no great difficulties to the understanding, no elaborate problems of interpretation, indeed, nothing but the task of literary judgment. What do we really feel, what is our true response, in reading *The Return of the Native?* I doubt that there is a single or simple answer, except perhaps for the wish to reclaim a book which Hardy's earlier admirers never dreamed would require anything but admiration.

The flaws are numerous and striking. One is disconcerted, first of all, by the pretentiousness of Hardy's style, his need, so painfully characteristic of the autodidact, to spread forth a glitter of artistic and literary references (as in his remark that Eustacia's "lips formed, with almost geometric precision, the curve so well known in the arts as the cima-recta, or ogee." Ogee indeed!) If there is one important Hardy novel that justifies the cruelty of T. S. Eliot's judgment that his style touched "sublimity without ever having passed through the stage of being good," it is *The Return of the Native.* Yet together with pasteboard flashiness there is, repeatedly, a passage of sublimity. The sounds of the heath, writes Hardy, formed a distinctive note, "what may be called" its "linguistic peculiarity":

> Throughout the blowing of these plaintive November winds that note bore a great resemblance to the ruins of human song which remain to the throat of four-score and ten. It was a worn whisper, dry and papery, and it brushed so distinctly across the ear that, by the accustomed, the material minutiae in which it originated could be realized as by touch.

It soon becomes evident that if the book is to yield any pleasure one must simply accept, as a recurrent irritation, Hardy's straining toward a brilliant stylized prose quite beyond his capacity and at odds with his most authentic gifts. But even at its worst, this impulse toward set-piece bravado is little more than an irritation: Hardy's failures, like his achievements, cannot be grasped by citing a few sentences.

To the subject of *The Return of the Native,* Hardy brings a somewhat fitful energy, so that the book seems ripely fulfilled in some parts and meagerly sketched in others. There are scenes in which the writing blazes with dramatic force and a marvelously frank speech (almost always when Mrs. Yeobright's dry anger flames into argument with the younger people). There are scenes in which the writing declines into a curious somnolence, as if it came from a novelist who sleep-writes the way some people sleep-walk. Except for *Tess of the D'Urbervilles,* this trouble will recur in all of Hardy's books, with rich detail and perfunctory synopsis repeatedly jostling each other. And one consequence, in *The Return of the Native,* is that crucial elements of intent and motive—what precisely is the cause of the estrangement between Clym and Eustacia?—seem to have been overlooked. To read the book is somewhat like watching a play for which the lighting works erratically, at one moment too glaring and another too weak.

Behind these troubles there is, one suspects, a confusion of literary purpose. The novel is blocked out—the novel as a scheme of situations and meanings—requires an action largely realistic, since it focuses upon a conflict of personal styles which, to gain their full value, must be presented through an opposition of social allegiances. What seems—I say "seems" because Hardy does not provide sufficient dramatic evidence—to be involved in the marital struggle between Clym and Eustacia is the problem of how men should live, by what standards, toward what ends. This kind of struggle, to be defined with maximum clarity, has to be located in a structured historical circumstance and organized about a specific social difficulty. Now Hardy seems very much aware of what that difficulty might be (as in his description of Clym as a man in whom "thought is a disease of the flesh"), but what he does not have available is a plot sufficiently complex and sustained to carry his awareness to its limits. The plot does not absorb and employ enough of Hardy's materials, too much is left hanging in mere remarks and fragments of incident; and the result is that one is constantly forced to notice the discrepancy between what happens and what the happenings are supposed to signify. Since the plot is, so to speak, too weak for the subject, there is no choice but to make a somewhat embarrassing reduction in one's mind as to the scope of the book. One thinks of it less and less as a novel charged with ideas about social restlessness and disorganization, more and more as a romance confined to a triangle of passionate misunderstandings.

To fill out his plot, Hardy falls back upon the rustics. By now these charming puppets have been so well trained, they can go through their act whenever Hardy curls a finger. But since he is not content to keep them as atmospheric diversion and must entangle them in his plot, Hardy burdens the rustics with responsibilities beyond their capacity to bear. Crucial turnings in the plot—for example, the whole painful misunderstanding that cuts off Mrs. Yeobright from the son she hoped to assuage—depend upon the rustics, as a result of which these figures are now transformed into agents of fate and chance. But because of what they are intrinsically—creatures, Albert Guerard notes, originally conceived as "immune to suffering and change"—they have a way of deflecting attention from the severity of the cosmic order and toward the inadequacy of the novelist's imagination. It is as if the low-comedy characters of *A Midsummer Night's Dream* were suddenly thrust into the milieu of *Madame Bovary*.

The best things in the novel are not sustained developments of realistic action and social detail, nor the overpraised descriptions of the heath, which seems closer to theater than to nature; they are incidents bordering on the grotesque. In most of his important novels Hardy was a writer struggling toward expressionist and symbolist fiction at a time when the only tradition immediately available to him was the conventional realism of the nineteenth century. In his later books he papered over these difficulties, and once or twice, certainly in *Tess,* found an action that helped release his deepest impulses as a writer. But I doubt that he ever quite solved the problem, except insofar as he abandoned prose fiction altogether and turned to verse, where he did not have to keep grappling with difficulties of plot and could content himself with the glancing effects of the vignette.

The vignettes of which I speak are often marvelous, coming as brief moments of illumination, usually when either Eustacia or Mrs. Yeobright ensnares a character in her passions. The book has another kind of power: long after one has brushed aside the passages of mannered or dead prose, one keeps in mind Hardy's central fable, a design of fatality resting on a triangle of mother, son, wife. I wish to distinguish here between plot, which is the form or curve of the action, and fable, which is the bare situation or dynamic of the characters. Most of the time, in *The Return of the Native,* plot is inadequate to fable. But the fable itself survives as a pure outline of human possibility, the conception behind the confusion.

Reading the novel one finds oneself thinking now and again: *here is a man who knows, who has seen and felt.* Many of the usual concerns of the nineteenth-century novel—articulated conflicts of class, differentiations of manners, the workings of society as a complex but self-contained organism—are barely evident in Hardy's fiction. The ethical dilemmas that absorb George Eliot, the nuances of conduct that trouble Henry James, the abysses of nihilism that haunt Joseph Conrad are largely beyond Hardy's reach. Compared to such writers he seems simple, crude, rough; but also full of an instinctive wisdom, an enormous weight of experience and reflection.

Hardy had an almost preternatural grasp of the dominant human passions, those which rip and tear our lives. He draws these passions with bold, unmodulated strokes—Mrs. Yeobright raging against her daughter-in-law, Clym mourning the death of his mother. The characterization is block-like, unshaded, monochromatic. Hardy reaches intuitively toward the few basic facts of human psychology and does not trouble to modulate or muddy them with psychological analysis. Usually his figures are in the grip of a single desire: Eustacia to realize romantic fantasies about herself, Clym to graft upon his life some significant purpose, Mrs. Yeobright to cling to the prerogatives of motherhood. What goes on within the minds of these figures we seldom know, nor need to. Our attention is directed not to their inner selves but to the stylized relationships among them, and the psychology of it all emerges not through a worrying of private scruples but through an almost ritualistic pattern of yearning, risk, nemesis and fate. The characters of *The Return of the Native* are not to be measured by the familiar standards of realistic probability: that is a test not many of them would pass. They are too large in scale, too singular in purpose to fit comfortably into the usual social novel. Like figures in traditional romance or ballad, they are embodiments of a ruling passion, or like figures in modernist fiction, they are agents of a tyrannical obsession. They live out their destinies, they die.

These people of Wessex, writes D. H. Lawrence,

> are always bursting suddenly out of bud and taking a wild flight into flower, always shooting suddenly out of a tight convention, a tight hide-bound cabbage state into something quite madly personal . . . it is all explosive . . . This is the tragedy of Hardy, always the same: the tragedy of those who, more or less pioneers, have died in the wilderness, whither they had escaped for free action, after having left the walled security, and the comparative imprisonment, of the established convention. This is the theme of novel after novel: remain quite within the convention, and you are good, safe and happy in the long run, though you never have the vivid pang of sympathy on your side; or, on the other hand, be passionate, individual, wilful, you will find the security of the convention a walled prison, you will escape, and you will die, either of your own lack of strength to bear the isolation and the exposure, or by direct revenge from the community, or both.

Yet if the central matter of *The Return of the Native* is a conflict between figures of convention and figures of rebellion, it can also be regarded as a struggle for the soul of a man who is not strong enough to shape his destiny or prevent his women from misshaping it. This struggle takes place between Eustacia, the smoldering country Delilah, and Mrs. Yeobright, a grim and perceptive woman, but in her willfulness not perceptive enough. Representing the rival claims of sensuality and constraint, these two women hover over Clym and allow him no peace. Gradually the thin substance of his manliness gets worn down. Clym's partial blindness is brought on by himself, an instance of that self-destructiveness which courses through the major characters and is regarded by Hardy as inseparable from the fevers of romanticism. But the decay of Clym's sight also suggests a diminished virility. Eustacia need not shear the locks of this fretful husband, who can at best be stubborn when his need is to be strong; it is quite enough that he declines into a leaden figure doing his mindless chores and withdrawing into heavy sexless sleep.

To have conceived Clym Yeobright, one of the earliest characters in English literature dominated by modern deracination and a hunger for some nameless purposes, was surely a triumph. Had Hardy known what to do with Clym in the actual course of the novel, his triumph would have been considerably greater. It is a common response and, I think, a correct one to see Clym as far too dim and recessive for the role Hardy assigns him. In first catching sight of what Clym means, Hardy could not yet see him clearly or fully enough to work him into a living action. Hardy's remarks about Clym are very acute, far more than anything he shows Clym himself to be doing or thinking. Often we have to take Hardy's word for it—since he does not adequately show us—that Clym is the kind of man who could win a girl as passionate and willful as Eustacia. The point is not that we fail to see why Eustacia should be drawn to a young man of some cultivation, just back from Paris and with a decidedly superior personal style. Here Hardy's psychology is very sharp, since it is precisely the destructiveness, and self-destructiveness, of a Eustacia that she should dream of satisfying her fantasies of worldly brilliance through a connection with a man of intellectual seriousness. There is a certain, though limited, comparison to be made with the marriage of Lydgate and Rosamund in *Middlemarch,* where a young girl's desire for worldly status also attaches itself to a man who begins without worldly ambition. But the concreteness of observed detail George Eliot could bring to her portrait of Lydgate, the care and patience with which she traced his gradual enslavement in domestic philistinism, are precisely what Hardy cannot bring to his rendering of Clym. We respond to Clym's dilemma more than to Clym; we see him as a possibility, a fictional forerunner more than a completed figure—though there are moments when he *is* strongly present, as in the scene where he sleeps heavily after his work at the furze-cutting, a man sliding into apathy. In the main, however, Clym is an idea, evidence of Hardy's stabbing insight, not a character grasped and realized.

Eustacia, by contrast, rises above the novel like a young goddess of sensuality, also like a young girl of petulant vanity. A bit larger than life, she is partly decked out in papier-mâché, and the falseness of it is utterly right. She knows the power of her beauty, but lacks any vision that might enable her to put it to more than trivial use. She quivers with the force of her sexuality, but what she wants most is a carriage in Paris. She has a fine mind, but wastes it on Wildeve, telescopes and daydreams. She harbors fantasies of a great and unconventional triumph, but the stuff from which she compounds these fantasies is utterly commonplace. "She had advanced," writes Hardy with quiet exactness, "to the secret recesses of sensuousness, yet had hardly crossed the threshold of the conventional." A "Queen of Night" in the somewhat lurid seventh chapter, she is also a poor befuddled young thing, trying painfully to impress the young gentleman from Paris. ("What depressed you?" asks Clym in their first conversation; "Life," replies Eustacia.) Her portrait is done in colors of grandeur, yet with at least a few specks of irony.

Clym cannot cope with her, either as a character in the story or as a force counterposed to him in the dialectic of the book. Only Mrs. Yeobright can, and we are grateful for the old lady, without whom there would be no astringency and little conflict. In my own experience of the novel Mrs. Yeobright keeps growing in force, this gritty puritan woman who alternates between passionate outbursts of self-assertion and sudden lapses into country stoicism. Surely Mrs. Yeobright served D. H. Lawrence as a model for the still more powerful Mrs. Morel in *Sons and Lovers*. In both of these mothers the thrust of will, the resources of age and the tyranny of experience frighten away the eager young girls loved by their sons. Fully achieved, Mrs. Yeobright comes out of Hardy's knowledge of Wessex particulars, but with a resonance more nearly universal.

These three figures meet in a struggle of wills, each pitting his or her stubbornness against the other, and the battle that follows, impressive as it is, really has little to do with the themes that have been adumbrated at the outset. Not Clym and the diseases of modernity, but the timeless rage of the clash between generations, the old clinging and the young grasping, provides the drama of the book.

It is in this perspective that we must see the problem of chance and coincidence, so troubling to Hardy's critics and sometimes even to his readers. No amount of critical ratiocination can—and more important, none should—dissolve this problem, for if we experience it as a difficulty in the reading of Hardy's novels, we must accept it as a problem in thinking about them. Yet there may be ways of controlling the difficulty. Chance and coincidence are used repeatedly in *The Return of the Native,* and the readers untrained to a large allowance of probability in fiction are likely to be troubled. But we must learn to bring expectations to the reading of Hardy different from those we bring to George Eliot or Jane Austen or Stendhal, for books like *The Return of the Native* deal less with the logic of the probable than the power of the implausible as it is made, now and again, to seem inevitable. Hardy believed in chance and coincidence, both as manifestations of fate and as signs revealing the dynamics of character. When Wildeve fails to get the marriage certificate, Mrs. Yeobright remarks, "Such things don't happen for nothing." She is right. Hardy is trying to say through the workings of chance what later writers will try to say through the vocabulary of the unconscious. The same holds true for Mrs. Yeobright's decision not to give the money to Wildeve but to entrust it to an unreliable yokel. It is apparently a chance act precipitating a series of disasters, but also another instance of Mrs. Yeobright's damaging pride and aggressiveness. Most of the chance events in the novel can be explained in such terms, which is not to suggest that all of them can thereby be justified or accepted.

Hardy is seldom a moralist. He watches over the men and women of Wessex with an almost maternal sympathy, as if he were a voice from the depths of time rehearsing the endless alternation of effort and collapse, desire and denial, rebellion and defeat. In the light of eternity, the impulse to moral judgment seems not very important. What matters in Hardy's world is the large and recurrent rhythms of life, the rhythms of happiness and suffering—and then, the small immediate incidents into which these are dramatically compressed. I think of the moment when Eustacia, as the result of a quarrel, prepares to leave Clym:

> At last all her things were on. Her little hands quivered so violently as she held them to her chin to fasten her bonnet that she could not tie the strings, and after a few moments she relinquished the attempt. Seeing this he moved forward and said, "Let me tie them."

In that one fragment, as it displays the force of habit in marriage at the very moment of its dissolution, Hardy caught the essence of human pain. Only a great novelist can fully apprehend such a moment, and only a great novelist can make it seem emblematic of our life.

The Return of the Native: A Novel of Environment

Jean R. Brooks

The Return of the Native strikes a harsher note than *Far from the Madding Crowd*. Egdon Heath, the resistant matter of the cosmos on which the action takes place, bears, shapes, nourishes, and kills conscious organisms possessed of its striving will without its unconsciousness of suffering. The six main characters take their key from Egdon. They all feel its pull through some affinity of temperament. Clym, Mrs Yeobright, and Diggory Venn share its look of isolation; Thomasin, Clym, and Venn its endurance; Eustacia and Wildeve, though they hate it, share its primal vitality and indifference to others. The rustics, too, take a more subdued tone from the heath. The accent of their talk falls on time passing, change, and decay. Their environment is one in which change and chance, death and darkness, prevail, and "the overpowering of the fervid by the inanimate" is a recognized conclusion to human effort.

It is fashionable in this denigrating age to decry Hardy's description of the heath in chapter 1 as pretentious. An earlier critic was nearer the mark in likening it to the entry of the Gods in Wagner. Large orchestras are not out of place in making the power of cosmic forces felt on the pulse. Egdon is presented as a visual correlative of space and time and the modern view of life "as a thing to be put up with." It is characteristic of Hardy's poetic style to begin with the specific—"A Saturday afternoon in November"—and widen the local view gradually to a philosophic vision of cosmic processes which the heath has power to affect:

From *Thomas Hardy: The Poetic Structure*. © 1971 by Jean R. Brooks. Elek Books, 1971.

> The face of the heath by its mere complexion added half an hour to evening; it could in like manner retard the dawn, sadden noon, anticipate the frowning of storms scarcely generated, and intensify the opacity of a moonless midnight to a cause of shaking and dread.

The description of the heath in terms of a face, "a face on which time makes but little impression," which will later be recalled by the face (Clym's) on which time has recorded disillusive experience, introduces the theme of shape that opposes the chaos of Egdon's primal matter. But in this first chapter the details emphasize storm and darkness. Jungians will recognize in Hardy's hint of the tragic climax the subconscious hinterland of elemental myth that present man's painful predicament in relation to a demonic landscape of barren earth, isolating wind, stormy water, and creative/destructive fire.

> The storm was its lover, and the wind its friend. Then it became the home of strange phantoms; and it was found to be the hitherto unrecognized original of those wild regions of obscurity which are vaguely felt to be compassing us about in midnight dreams of flight and disaster, and are never thought of after the dream till revived by scenes like this.

Its "Titanic form" widens the perspective still further to invest the heath with heroic echoes of classical myth; particularly the Prometheus myth of rebellion against darkness. There is a swing back again, characteristic of Hardy's poetic method, from these long philosophical perspectives to "intelligible facts regarding landscape," its emotional and practical connection with man and his efforts to civilize it. The evocation ends with another swing from localized human vision to a vista of geological aeons. The Latinate dignity of the language, the balanced pauses, the unhurried rhythm, the slow buildup of paragraph structure, enact a persistent hammering at intractable physical substance which is part of the character and theme of Egdon.

> The great inviolate place had an ancient permanence which the sea cannot claim. Who can say of a particular sea that it is old? Distilled by the sun, kneaded by the moon, it is renewed in a year, in a day, or in an hour. The sea changed, the fields changed, the rivers, the villages, and the people changed, yet Egdon remained. Those surfaces were neither so steep as to be destructible by weather, nor so flat as to be the victims of floods and deposits.

> With the exception of an aged highway, and a still more aged barrow . . . themselves almost crystallized to natural products by long continuance —even the trifling irregularities were not caused by pickaxe, plough, or spade, but remained as the very finger-touches of the last geological change.

The Return of the Native is concerned with the Promethean struggle of conscious life against the unconscious "rayless" universe from which it sprang. The poetic-dramatic structure of the first chapters initiates the underlying metaphor of the novel, the ancient conflict of light and darkness. The white man-made road that crosses the brown heath, the red glow of bonfires, the "blood-coloured" figure of Diggory Venn, challenge the dark drabness of the earth.

> To light a fire is the instinctive and resistant act of man when, at the winter ingress, the curfew is sounded throughout Nature. It indicates a spontaneous, Promethean rebelliousness against the fiat that this recurrent season shall bring foul times, cold darkness, misery and death. Black chaos comes, and the fettered gods of the earth say, Let there be light.

The almost supernatural figure of Diggory Venn modulates between the heath and the human beings whose desire for joy and purpose troubles the scene. He is dyed into an identification of the heath and its products. Yet his conspicuous fiery colour suggests a character that will master reality through involvement with it.

Chapter 2 begins with one of Hardy's familiar images of the human condition, the meeting of two lonely figures on a deserted road. One wonders about the meaning of the two walking figures and the woman concealed in the van. The chapter ends with another anonymous figure rising from the central point of Rainbarrow as the apex of plain, hill, and tumulus. Between the two scenes of human interest stands the modulating chord of the heath. Hardy is careful to plant his descriptions of scene where they will direct emotion. The reader's eye is forced to follow the reddleman's musing survey upwards from the "speck on the road" that defines the vanishing Captain to the protruberance of the barrow and the ambiguous potential of the crowning figure to make or mar human significance.

The shifting perspective, that enlarges and diminishes the human figure ("a pike from a helmet," "the only obvious justification of [the hills'] outline," "it descended . . . with the glide of a water-drop down a bud"), and transforms the barrow itself from "a wart on an Atlantean brow" to "the pole and axis of this heathery world," leaves in suspension the comparative significance of scene and human actors. The figure of unknown potential has been associated with the Celts who built the barrow as a bulwark of order against chaos; but what it marks is a place of death. It gives a perfect aesthetic finish to the mass; yet the Greek ideal of perfect beauty has been defined in chapter 1 as an anachronism. As it disappears, the surprise of the movement where all seemed fixity stresses the function of human consciousness on the natural scene. It can change and be changed.

Change is the keynote of the distance "sky-backed pantomime of silhouettes" which replaces the composition of barrow and lonely figure. In chapter 3 the focus shifts from the permanent mass of the heath, with solitary wanderers crawling like ants over its surface and the still figure on its central point, to a firelit impression of movement and evanescence.

> All was unstable; quivering as leaves, evanescent as lightning. Shadowy eye-sockets, deep as those of a death's head, suddenly turned into pits of lustre: a lantern-jaw was cavernous, then it was shining; wrinkles were emphasized to ravines, or obliterated entirely by a changed ray.

Stillness gives way to motion; the solitary figure reaching for the sky to several "burdened figures" bowed down under the furze they carry, playing out the next stage of human development. The pyramid-shaped bonfire they build to top the barrow enacts a wordless ritual of human function to shape and control. The heath, detached from them by the radiant circle of light they have created, becomes the "vast abyss" of Milton's, Dante's, and Homer's hell. By implication, the distorted human features evoke tormented souls acting out a timeless doom.

Hardy modulates from ritual to the human plane by bringing the fragmented Grandfer Cantle gradually forward from the composition to speak and act as a mortal limited by time and the need for warmth and self-assertion. The elemental ritual of light and darkness recedes as the kindly rustic voices gather strength. But it remains in the imagination of colour the talk of local human concerns with its larger rhythms. The conflict of wills that emerges from the gossip about Mrs Yeobright forbidding the banns, Tamsin's rash choice of Wildeve, Wildeve's character and attainments, the criticism of Eustacia's noncommunal bonfire, the anticipation of Clym's Promethean role—"What a dog he used to be for bonfires!"—the nostalgia for youth and quiet acceptance of death as part of the seasonal cycle: all are marked with the preceding evocation of the limitations of the earth and the desire to transcend them; the fire of life and passion and the distortion of reality it brings with its comfort; the double vision of man's speck-like insignificance on the face of the heath and the poetic light that gives his ephemeral features the eternal grandeur of ravines and caverns.

The human drama evolves, as it were, from the scene and its implications. The character of Egdon encourages resistance and determines the kind of action that can take place within its bounds. Isolation fosters Eustacia's attraction to Clym and to a man of inferior calibre, the misunderstanding between Clym and his mother, the misapprehension about Mrs Yeobright's guineas. The openness of the country enables bonfire signals to be seen for miles; and kills Mrs Yeobright after her exhausting walk from one isolated cottage to another. Much of the action consists of solitary journeys across the heath to keep up communications or assignations, to spy out the land, or pursue erring mortals who have lost their way literally and figuratively on the dark crisscrossing paths that become symbolic of their antagonistic purposes. The presence of the vast passionless heath puts the human movements into perspective as the scurrying of ephemeral ants.

The plot resembles *Far from the Madding Crowd* in the tragic chain of love relationships and the situation of Wildeve, the gay man vacillating between the innocent girl he is engaged to and the woman of greater passion and complexity. The pattern is again complicated by an idealist with an obsession, though Clym Yeobright's ambition, unlike Boldwood's, is unconnected with the irrational force of sexual love. Mrs Yeobright adds another colour to the figure in the carpet in the conflict between generations and their ideals of progress. As usual, the poetic stylization contributes to meaning. Douglas Brown notes that

> the very grouping of the protagonists tells much. On one far side is Thomasin ("All similes concerning her began and ended with birds") and on the other, Wildeve, the ineffectual engineer, invading the country to become a publican. Clym (the native home from exile) and Eustacia (seeking exile, and confusing that with home) stand between them. At the centre, between Clym and Eustacia, Mrs Yeobright is subtly placed, a countrywoman upholding urban attitudes whose true nature and effect she cannot perceive.

R. W. Stallman, in his ingenious article "Hardy's Hour-Glass Novel" (*The Sewanee Review* 55 [1947]) sees in the novel a chain of seven "hour-glass" plots, in which Fate keeps turning the hourglass over to reverse events, situations, and partners.

The tragic action was designed originally to lead to the double death in the weir, involving the earlier tragedy of Mrs Yeobright's death. The original five-part structure, the strict regard for unities of place, time (the year and a day of folklore quest), and action, may recall Shakespearean and classical drama. The two signal fires are the novel's poles of time and action, and Rainbarrow its axis in space. But such stylization is part of Hardy's normal poetic technique. The five parts clearly graph the stages in the interrelated love affairs, and the disillusionment which reality brings to Eustacia's romantic dreams of happiness and Clym's dreams of finding a purpose.

Book 1 introduces the three women whose relationship to the two men is to promote a tragic antagonism of ideals. The wedding complications of Tamsin and Wildeve introduce the blind obstructiveness of things (the marriage licence, and the subconscious reluctance of Wildeve that allowed the mistake to happen; Mrs Yeobright's "Such things don't happen for nothing" anticipates the psychology of Freudian error), and the countermoves of human intelligence (Mrs Yeobright's unscrupulous use of Venn as a rival lover to bring Wildeve to heel, and Venn's active determination to look after Tamsin's interests). Book 2, "The Arrival," resolves the marriage complications and changes the emotional current by the return of Clym Yeobright. Interest is sustained by the potential of conflict and attraction between a man who has rejected the worldly vanity of Paris and a woman for whom he represents an avenue of escape to its delights. Book 3, "The Fascination," charts the blind sexual attraction between Clym and Eustacia, each a distorted projection of fulfilment to the other, and the serious division it causes between Clym and his mother. Mrs Yeobright's attempt to heal the breach by her gift of money to Tamsin and Clym sows the seeds of the catastrophe by a combination of carelessness (she entrusts the money to the weak-witted Christian Cantle), blind chance (Wildeve wins the guineas from Cantle), and ignorance (Venn does not know that half the money he wins back from Wildeve was destined for Clym).

Book 4, "The Closed Door," shows more than one door closing on human possibilities. Clym's blindness limits his ambitions to knowledge of a few square feet of furze. Simultaneously it dashes Eustacia's hopes of escaping Egdon through Clym, and sends her back to Wildeve. Wildeve's presence in the cottage with Eustacia when Mrs Yeobright calls keeps the door closed against her, and Clym's heavy sleep is another closed door. Hope of reconciliation is closed for ever by Mrs Yeobright's lonely death on the heath. But Johnny Nunsuch's dramatic restatement of Mrs Yeobright's words, "she said I was to say that I had seed her, and she was a broken-hearted woman and cast off by her son" opens the door to Clym's painful discovery in Book 5 of the circumstances of her death and Eustacia's part in it. "The Discovery" charts the steps Clym takes to find out the truth, and the Oedipus-like irony that each step he takes drives him deeper into a hell of remorse, self-knowledge, and division from the other woman he loves. The final step drives Eustacia from his anger to seek escape through Wildeve, and to a despairing death with him in storm and darkness.

Hardy gave way to editorial necessity and common probability to add Book 6, which presents "the inevitable movement onward" that restores order after tragic catastrophe. Tamsin and Diggory Venn find happiness in marriage, and Clym partial fulfilment as an itinerant preacher, to the accompaniment of the rituals of May Day and the waxing of a feather bed for the married pair, which involve them all in the seasonal rite of fertility and regeneration.

One can point to the usual incidents in the working out of plot which compel comparisons vital to structure. The different purposes, selfish and altruistic, which motivate the characters to seek conflicting manifestations of fulfilment; which animate the various figures who crown Rainbarrow, and inspire the lonely journeys taken across the heath, are worth close study. The different attitudes to Egdon and its limitations and traditions are embodied, as Dr. Beatty has shown, in Hardy's descriptions of Mistover Knap and Blooms-End. Captain Vye's house at Mistover Knap has "the appearance of a fortification." Blooms-End is separated from the heath only by a row of white palings and a little garden (which orders nature by control, not defence). The traditional mummers find a warm welcome at Blooms-End, the family home of the Yeobrights; while "for mummers and mumming Eustacia had the greatest contempt." At Blooms-End, the loft over the fuel-house "was lighted by a semicircular hole, through which the pigeons crept to their lodgings in the same high quarters of the premises," and the sun irradiated Tamsin as she selected apples from their natural packing of fern, with "pigeons . . . flying about her head with the greatest unconcern." At the fuel-house of Mistover Knap, the outsider Eustacia looks in from the darkness at the mummers' rehearsal to relieve her boredom, through "a small rough hole in the mud wall, originally made for pigeons," but now disused, and the building is lit from the inside.

What the contrasts reveal is that all the stylizations draw their meaning from the underpattern of conflicting light and dark. This central opposition moves the conflict between Clym and Eustacia, to which all the other characters stand in dramatic relationship. Their association with the elemental forces in conflict is defined by the fire and light images which identify them with the Promethean myth, and the images of darkness and death that endow Eustacia additionally with some of the attributes of Persephone Queen of the Shades.

The different manifestations of light and fire which define the characters also define their responses to the leitmotif question "What is doing well?" Wildeve has the "curse of inflammability"; Eustacia is a smouldering subterranean fire reaching by blind instinct for the suns; they snatch at the heat of momentary passion in a rebellion that speaks to the twentieth-century rebellion against the permanence of things. Clym's way of opposing the gods of darkness is to bring light rather than fire to mankind. (The name "Yeobright" is significant in both its parts.) Tamsin is marked by the image of benevolent sunshine. Mrs Yeobright, who has ignored the primitive power of the cosmos in her "civilized" desires for Clym's advancement, meets death by fire in a parched waste land with a poisonous serpent and a sun that foreshadows the hostile antagonist of Camus's *The Outsider.* Diggory Venn is permeated with the colour of fire, and shares the craft and symbolic ambiguity of the early fire-god Loki. Fire as an answer to darkness can be creative or destructive; an instrument of mastery or chaos. The scenes that carry the underpattern show the characters acting out their ritual roles as bringers of light or darkness to the pattern of human fate.

Clym Yeobright plays the double role of Promethean hero and ironic parody of primitive heroic attitudes. There is no doubt about his altruistic Promethean aspirations. "The deity that lies ignominiously chained within an ephemeral human carcase shone out of him like a ray." His absence has taught him that Egdon realities are realities the world over. Yet the context in which we first see Clym at close quarters (bk. 2, chap. 6) qualifies our approval of his aim to teach the Egdon eremites "how to breast the misery they are born to." At the Blooms-End Christmas party the snug picture framed by the settle does not show much evidence of misery.

> At the other side of the chimney stood the settle, which is the necessary supplement to a fire so open that nothing less than a strong breeze will carry up the smoke. It is, to the hearths of old-fashioned cavernous fireplaces, what the east belt of trees is to the exposed country estate, or the north wall to the garden. Outside the settle candles gutter, locks of hair wave, young women shiver, and old men sneeze. Inside is Paradise. Not a symptom of a draught disturbs the air; the sitters' backs are as warm as their faces, and songs and old tales are drawn from the occupants by the comfortable heat, like fruit from melon-plants in a frame.

Hardy's selection of concrete detail to build up poetic mood and sequence takes us from the physical effects of the coldness outside to the simple statement that sums up human yearning for fulfilment, "Inside was

Paradise." The simile of melon-plants in a frame clinches the natural sequence of comfort and growth that order this earthly Paradise—which Clym would jump in his ascetic plans for higher development.

> To argue upon the possibility of culture before luxury to the bucolic world may be to argue truly, but it is an attempt to disturb a sequence to which humanity has been long accustomed.

Outside the ordered frame of unreflective comfort are Clym, who has passed beyond it, and Eustacia, who has not yet reached it. The conjunction of traditional scene of conviviality, blind animal will to enjoy that has motivated Eustacia's presence, and Clym's "typical countenance of the future" marked by consciousness of man's tragic predicament in an uncaring universe, questions whether modern perceptiveness may be an unmixed blessing to men untouched by the disillusive centuries and adapted to the world they live in.

Clym's troubles spring from his failure to respect the laws of physical reality. His blindness is both a natural consequence of ignoring physical strain on his eyes, a simplification of the modern complexity of life which denies him "any more perfect insight into the conditions of existence," and a complex poetic symbol of the figurative blindness displayed by this representative of "modern perceptiveness" who "loved his kind," to the needs of the individuals closest to him, and to the nature of his illusions. He is blind to the reality which is in the heath, himself, his mother, Eustacia, and the "Egdon eremites" he had come to teach how to bear it. He meets its obstructiveness in the common resistance to the kind of progress that jumps the stage of social advance, in the irrational demands of sexual love, in the reality of Eustacia's primitive nature that runs counter to his projected image of her (a fault that makes him brother to Angel Clare and Knight). His sense of affinity with the dead and virgin moonscape (bk. 3, chap. 4), and the appearance of the "cloaked figure" of Eustacia, who is repeatedly associated with night, death, and the moon, at the base of Rainbarrow simultaneously with the eclipse ("for the remote celestial phenomenon had been pressed into sublunary service as a lover's signal") are correlative to his destructive and self-destructive attachment to Absolute Reality.

The failure of Clym's Promethean aim leads one to consider his role as an ironic reversal of the traditional hero-myth. R. Carpenter, in *Thomas Hardy,* sees the heroic archetype in Clym's quest for meaning. His originality is recognized at an early age, he serves his apprenticeship in a foreign land guarding treasure, and becomes possessed of deeper knowledge which he wishes to pass on to his people. His temporary withdrawal from the world suggests the initiation of a sun-god-hero into a religious cult. He returns to his birthplace, a dark and fallen world (Tartarus, the prison of the exiled Titans) but is not really recognized. He is diverted from his quest by a dark and beautiful enchantress against the wishes of his goddess mother, undergoes a period of spiritual trial and is symbolically blinded, like Oedipus and Milton's Samson, so that he may achieve true insight. The counterpointing strain of the hero who triumphs over obstacles to shape destiny, questions the validity, to the modern mind aware of "the obstructive coil of things," of simple heroic resistance. To Louis Crompton Clym is a compound of the free hero of romance, the hero of classical tragedy, subject to fate and moral judgement, whose hubris leads to his downfall, and the diminished hero of modern realism, subject to biological and economic laws which limit human responsibility. But the wry comment on ancient heroic standards should not hide the genuine heroism achieved by a man who must painfully scale down his notions of progress to the limitations that condition the slow rate of evolutionary change. ("This was not the repose of actual stagnation, but the apparent repose of incredible slowness.")

The new concept of heroic action redefines Clym's quest as the quest of fallen man to reestablish harmony with nature. Clym takes his first steps towards Paradise regained when he accepts his primitive roots, puts on his old brown clothes, and becomes of no more account than a parasitic insect fretting the surface of the heath. Knowledge is redefined, in a poetic passage that emphasizes each unit of the physical scene with a major stress and pause, as "having no knowledge of anything in the world but fern, furze, heath, lichens, and moss." His movements over the heath, feeling, sensing through the dark, bring an intense regenerative contact with the physical world that is a source of strength in misery, even though conscious man can never achieve complete harmony. Hardy's description of Clym working among the small heath creatures, with its details of colour and movement, its varying rhythms of natural activity, its acceptance of the sun's meaning as simple warmth and beauty for the earth's creatures, its delight in vitality, and its superbly simple climax, celebrates like his poetry an enlargement of the horizon within those limited areas where man can still find certainty.

> His daily life was of a curious microscopic sort, his whole world being limited to a circuit of a few feet from his person. His familiars were creeping and winged things, and they seemed to enrol him in their band. Bees hummed around his ears with an intimate air, and tugged at the heath and furze-flowers at his side in such numbers as to weigh them down to the sod. The

> strange amber-coloured butterflies which Egdon produced, and which were never seen elsewhere, quivered in the breath of his lips, alighted upon his bowed back, and sported with the glittering point of his hook as he flourished it up and down. Tribes of emerald-green grasshoppers leaped over his feet, falling awkwardly on their backs, heads, or hips, like unskilful acrobats, as chance might rule; or engaged themselves in noisy flirtations under the fern-fronds with silent ones of homely hue. Huge flies, ignorant of larders and wire-netting, and quite in a savage state, buzzed about him without knowing that he was a man. In and out of the fern-dells snakes glided in their most brilliant blue and yellow guise, it being the season immediately following the shedding of their old skins, when their colours are brightest. Litters of young rabbits came out from their forms to sun themselves upon hillocks, the hot beams blazing through the delicate tissue of each thin-fleshed ear, and firing it to a blood-red transparency in which the veins could be seen. None of them feared him.

Clym has recently been demoted from protagonist, and Eustacia promoted, on the grounds that she has the heroic force which he lacks. But it is surely intentional that a character possessing the animal vitality of a more primitive era should make a greater sensuous impact than the new heroic type, "slighted and enduring," distinguished by contemplative rather than active heroism. The two characters are perfectly balanced in their vital opposition to carry the meaning of the story.

Eustacia's delineation as "Queen of Night" indicates her function as a reverse parallel to Clym. Her first and last appearance is on the barrow, house of the dead. She shares, while she suffers from, the heath's darkness, "Tartarean dignity," indifference, and slumbrous vitality. But her relation to Clym is not a simple opposition of darkness to light. It is also the antagonism of illumination at different stages of development.

The first sentence of chapter 7, book 1, where she is defined as Queen of Night, stresses the two qualities that associate her on one side with the heath and on the other with the Promethean Clym. "Eustacia Vye was the raw material of a divinity." Her animal nature, unreflecting and unpurposive ("she would let events fall out as they might sooner than wrestle to direct them") partakes of the blind chaos of the heath's raw material, which has not yet reached Promethean forethought. The many classical and romantic metaphors and the "geometric precision" of her perfect beauty define Eustacia as an anachronistic reincarnation of the Hellenic age whose "old-fashioned revelling in the general situation" is being replaced by the record of disillusive time (destroyer of beauty) that scars the other faces, of Clym and the heath. But the subterranean fire of divinity is there, chained to an ideal of fulfilment antagonistic to Clym's and out of tune with the haggard times.

Her poetic context in chapter 6 defines the sun she seeks for her soul. The cumulative evocation of the wind over the heath, that begins in distinguishing the special notes of the "infinitesimal vegetable causes" which harmonize to produce "the linguistic peculiarity of the heath," and rises to a philosophical contemplation of Infinity as it is made sensuously manifest in the sound of the combined multitudes of mummied heath-bells scoured by the wind, is a rich image that evokes simultaneously the timelessness of nonhuman time that diminishes human importance, against which Eustacia rebels, and the absolute loneliness that is the price of her god-like rejection of human compromise. Her challenge to the forces that render beauty ephemeral is "a blaze of love, and extinction, . . . better than a lantern glimmer . . . which should last long years," and a too thorough identification, suggested by hourglass and telescope, with the metaphysic of transience.

Eustacia's will to enjoy in the present moment is the universal thrust of life to grow out of the primal stage of blind, self-absorbed groping towards the sun to a state of being where light, form, and meaning are imposed on matter. But she is false to her humanity by acquiescing in the lower state, as Clym is false to his by wanting to jump the intermediate stage of evolution to reach the higher. Consequently her environment controls her as it controls the ear of corn in the ground. The two movements down from and up beyond the human norm meet in a god-like desire for absolute reality, which Hardy's poetic transformation of light into darkness define as a form of the death-wish.

Eustacia's dream (bk. 2, chap. 3) is the first of a series of related ritual enactments of her subconscious drive to self-destruction. A comparison with her mumming adventure, (bk. 2, chaps. 5, 6), the Egdon gipsying (bk. 4, chap. 3) and her death (bk. 5, chaps. 7–9) reveals the fantastic action of the dream ironically transformed and realized in a complex love/death sequence. The shining knight with whom she dances and plunges into the water is transformed from her Paradisal Clym to the commonplace Wildeve. The visor that hides his face turns into the mummers' ribbons that hide hers, as their true natures are concealed by their projected roles. The ecstatic dance becomes a Dionysiac revel that replaces a "sense of social order" with the self-destructive sexual impulse. The expected consummation under the pool is revealed first as her ritual death at the hands of the Christian Knight in the mummers' play, and finally as the real embrace of death with Wildeve in the weir, for which her ideal knight is partly responsible. The woman who feels she is in Paradise becomes the woman who is excluded, with Clym, from the earthly Paradise inside the settle. The brilliant rainbow light modulates to the moonlight of the mumming and the gipsying, the familiar illusory moonlight existence of Eustacia's imagination, which stresses the fantastic, trance-like ritual aspect of movement and mask-like features. It resolves finally into the hellish red glow from Susan Nunsuch's cottage that reveals the "splendid woman" who arraigns the Prince of the World as a mere waxen image of pride and vanity, and reconciles Eustacia's death by water to the death by fire consuming her in effigy. The heath that is only dimly felt in the dream looms larger and blacker in the following scenes to block her desire for absolute heroic existence. The shining knight who falls into fragments as the dreamer's translation of "the cracking . . . of the window-shutter downstairs, which the maid-servant was opening to let in the day," foreshadows the disintegration of her ideal world in face of the obstructive reality of Clym's nature and the world's daylight triviality. Her death sets her in her only "artistically happy background," where her conflicting drives to darkness and sunlight are reconciled. "Pallor did not include all the quality of her complexion, which seemed more than whiteness; it was almost light."

Clym and Eustacia each have a partial truth that bears on the question of how to live. Mrs Yeobright provides another. Her conception of doing well is coloured by Egdon, which she neither loves nor hates, but tries to ignore in her desire to civilize the wilderness. She is one of T. S. Eliot's women of Canterbury, fearful of the "disturbance of the quiet seasons" and human order from the ultimate powers of the cosmos which Clym and Eustacia know as light and heat and darkness.

Mrs Yeobright is related poetically to the heath and to the elemental struggle of light and darkness by Hardy's visual presentation. When she steps forward into the light of the bonfire in book 1, chapter 3, "her face, encompassed by the blackness of the receding heath, showed whitely, and without half-lights, like a cameo." The profile etched distinctly on a dark ground, repeated in our first sight of Clym's face (bk. 2, chap. 6) and Eustacia's (bk. 1, chap. 6) suggests inflexible resistance to cosmic darkness.

Her journey across the heath to her death builds up a complex poetic image of her confrontation by the ultimate reality of the cosmos which civilization does not cope with. Its absurdity and hostility to human purpose are demonstrated in the action of the closed door. Poetically, they are embodied in the merciless sun and the parched obstructive earth she has to cross; major symbols of the elemental conflict between Clym and Eustacia which destroys her in its working out. Every image, every word, is selected for sound and sense to evoke a harsh wasteland on fire with the blazing sun that "had branded the whole heath with his mark": the scorched and flagging plants, the air "like that of a kiln," the "incineration" of the quartz sand, the "metallic mirrors" of smooth-fleshed leaves, the moan of lightning-blasted trees. Echoes of Lear and his Fool on the stormy heath in Johnny Nunsuch's innocent questions and statements of fact and Mrs Yeobright's answers charged with experience of human misery, heighten the poetic emotion. But it is controlled by the changing perspective that measures Mrs Yeobright's human effort objectively against the lowly species of the heath "busy in all the fulness of life" and indifferent to her prostration.

> Independent worlds of ephemerons were passing their time in mad carousal, some in the air, some on the hot ground and vegetation, some in the tepid and stringy water of a nearly dried pool. All the shallower ponds had decreased to a vaporous mud amid which the maggoty shapes of innumerable obscure creatures could be indistinctly seen, heaving and wallowing with enjoyment.

Human isolation from primal harmony is complete. The "vaporous mud" and "maggoty shapes . . . heaving and wallowing" evoke a preconscious world in which human emotion and purpose are anachronisms. If these lowly creatures recall Eustacia's preconscious will to enjoy, the gleaming wet heron who flies towards the sun recalls the unworldly aspirations of Clym, equally antagonistic to Mrs Yeobright's desire for civilization. The ants who share with her the shepherd's-thyme where she lies dying, "where they toiled a never-ending and heavy-laden throng" in a miniature city street, define the futile bustle of her "doing well" in face of the sun, which "stood directly in her face, like some merciless incendiary, brand in hand, waiting to consume her."

Wildeve's relationship to Egdon and the Promethean light that rebels against it denotes a man who is not great enough to become a force of nature instead of a helpless instrument. Even his vices are petty; his little meannesses about Tamsin's allowance, his trumpery schemes of revenge. Our first sight of him through the window of the Quiet Woman is not of a sharp profile, but an indeterminate "vast shadow, in which could be dimly traced portions of a masculine contour." His tendency "to care for the remote, to dislike the near" recalls Eustacia's and Clym's dissatisfaction with human limitations. But Wildeve cannot initiate rebellion. He can only respond to Eustacia's fire, and be consumed in her flame, like the moth-signal he releases to her.

Tamsin Yeobright and Diggory Venn are grouped together to reflect the passive and active principle of acquiescence in the human condition that is Egdon. Tamsin, the gentle point of rest between the major antagonists, has no awkward ideas about doing well to thrust her out of her environment. Doing simply means marrying for Tamsin, and her firmness on this point helps to retrieve the error of the unfulfilled wedding that begins the novel. The sun-lighted ritual of braiding her hair on the wedding day stresses her adherence to the traditional ordering of birth, marriage, children, and death—one of the few ambitions that tally with the Egdon rate of progress. The images of light and music which introduce her (bk. 1, chap. 4) imply a relationship to the earth that has not yet become discordant. Benevolent sunshine is her natural form of light, but even on the night of storm and chaos which is a perfect complement to the chaos within Eustacia, Tamsin's sense of proportion and lack of that pride which demands a personal antagonist preserves her from harm.

> To her there were not, as to Eustacia, demons in the air, and malice in every bush and bough. The drops which lashed her face were not scorpions, but prosy rain; Egdon in the mass was no monster whatever, but impersonal open ground. Her fears of the place were rational, her dislikes of its worst moods reasonable.

Diggory Venn, acquiescing in human limitations while working at the same time, like Oak, with the grain of his environment, has a link with darkness and fire that is ambiguous. When action depends on intimate knowledge of the heath—when he uses the camouflage of turves to eavesdrop on the plans of Eustacia and Wildeve, or when his familiarity with Shadwater Wier enables him to devise a plan of rescue—his triumph is due to the light of human intelligence controlling human events. But his sudden appearances and disappearances, his colour, his devil's luck in gambling, his tricksy pranks with their unpredictable outcome, invest him with the poetry of a supernatural folklore character; not so much a "Mephistophilian visitant" of the Christian era as a primitive fire daemon capable of good or evil. John Hagan points out ("A Note on the Significance of Diggory Venn," *Nineteenth-Century Fiction,* 16, [1961–62]) that his well-intentioned interventions solve immediate problems, but initiate unwittingly the long-range tragedy of cosmic cross-purposes: Eustacia's decision to abandon Wildeve for Clym, and the events connected with the closed door.

Hardy's extended description of the reddleman stresses the ambiguity in his character which mirrors the ambiguity of the cosmos. The domestic picture (bk. 1, chap. 8) of a peaceful red man smoking a red pipe and darning a red stocking, kindly binding Johnny's wounds with a red bandage, gives way in chapter 9 to an evocation of his shadow side. His link with the heath is stressed in the "blood-coloured figure" which is, like Egdon in storm, "a sublimation of all the horrid dreams" of the human race. "Blood-coloured," an alteration from the simple "red" of the manuscript, takes up the theme of guilt suggested in "the mark of Cain" simile which defines the effects of reddle, and amplified in the evocation of the reddleman as an isolated "Ishmaelitish" character (the same adjective describes both the heath and the reddleman) who had taken to the trade as a lifelong penance for criminal deeds. The imaginative details of a legendary inheritance of guilt superimposed on the good and well-balanced human character of Diggory Venn suggest, paradoxically, a harmony with what Egdon means through acceptance of isolation and the guilt inherent in existence. After Clym's agonized self-reproach at Eustacia's death, it is Venn who puts it into perspective.

> "But you can't charge yourself with crimes in that way," said Venn. "You may as well say that the parents be the cause of a murder by the child, for without the parents the child would never have been begot."

The heightened poetic tone of chapter 8, book 3 where Venn wins back the Yeobright guineas, defines his ambiguous relation to light and darkness in a brilliant sensuous correlative. The overpowering darkness of the heath at night is fitfully broken by various forms of light which illuminate the flat stone, reminiscent of the flatness of the heath, and human participation in a game of chance, which becomes an image of the human predicament. It is natural that Venn's familiarity with the heath should give him an advantage over the excitable Wildeve, who is disturbed by the humbler heathdwellers. Wildeve's confused actions and Venn's calmness, chance, and direction, range themselves wtih the antagonisms of darkness and light that motivate the novel. The visual presentation of Venn as a "red automaton" raises him to the plane of a supernatural agent of fate. But his human lack of knowledge that half the guineas were destined for Clym qualifies his control of the situation.

The ritual patterns in the scene intensify its effect as a glimpse of destiny working itself out on another plane. In the heightened poetic tension, Venn's ballad-like incantation of the incremental phrases of Wildeve's gambling stories as the money coils in in reverse direction; the night moths which circle the lantern twice; the heath-croppers who encircle the gamblers twice, "their heads being all towards the players, at whom they gazed intently"; the thirteen glowworms placed in a circle round the dice, take on the aspect of mechanical functions of fate controlled by the "red automaton." The moths attracted to the light and the death's-head moth which extinguishes the lantern to the accompaniment of "a mournful whining from the herons which were nesting lower down the vale," foreshadow in symbol and detail the deaths of Wildeve and Mrs Yeobright.

The transformation of a folklore character into a mundane dairy farmer with a bank balance in book 6 worries some critics. While Hardy's note to chapter 3 indicates that his "austere artistic code" did not originally plan such a transformation, Venn's change tallies with the laws that condition Egdon's rate of progress. The cycle of aeons as well as the cycle of seasons directs his evolution from a "nearly perished link between obsolete forms of life and those which generally prevail." It is part of the movement of the novel from primitive darkness to conscious understanding appropriate to the modern era.

The poetic development of the novel is completed by a return to the visual image of "a motionless figure standing on the top of the tumulus, just as Eustacia had stood on that lonely summit some two years and a half before." But the transformation of Eustacia into Clym has replaced the dark winter night with summer afternoon, isolation with relationship to man and the lower species, and the self-absorbed unconscious drives of nature with hope of redemption through man's consciousness of the roots from which he sprang. Clym's suffering has taught him that love of place or woman is not enough without understanding, and that in order to move forward on Egdon one must move back.

To know Egdon is to know the great forces that move the world. It is not isolated from the rest of space, and time. Vapours from other continents arrive upon the wind, and rare migrants as well as native species watch the alien movements of man in a setting that "seemed to belong to the ancient carboniferous period." Egdon contains all the elements of the world before the Fall, including a secluded Paradise and a serpent. All its Promethean characters are seeking a place where they will feel at home after the development of isolating consciousness. Their survival depends on their reassessment of the place where they are. Hardy's sensuous evocation of the heath and its effect on human fate makes its physical presence impossible to ignore. At moments of crisis its "oppressive horizontality" gives Clym, and others, "a sense of bare equality with, and no superiority to, a single living thing under the sun." There is no special place in nature for man. But from the heath's dark negation springs that affirmation of its raw vitality and that yearning for the light which combine to enable conscious man, as part of the general Will, to

> Bend a digit the poise of forces,
> And a fair desire fulfil.
> ("He Wonders about Himself")

Eustacia Vye, Queen of Night and Courtly Pretender

David Eggenschwiler

The heroine of *The Return of the Native* is not quite as popular as she once was, at least as a heroine. Although most commentators still respond as readers always have to Eustacia's dark seductiveness, many also find her at times adolescent and foolish, and they compare her with Madame Bovary and Jane Austen's self-deluded young women. John Paterson, in fact, has shown that Hardy first conceived Eustacia as a less appealing character than she turned out to be after the author, too, became fascinated and gave her tragic proportions. But not all critics are as generous as Paterson in evaluating Hardy's mixed conceptions. Most recently, Robert Evans has charged the novel with being basically confused; he claims that Hardy tried to suggest a tragic heroine through a "pasteboard of rhetoric" but that he actually created a "selfish, immature, incurably romantic" girl, the truth about whom "the reader wins through to in spite of Hardy, not because of him."

I agree that the novel does show and even demand conflicting attitudes toward Eustacia, but I do not find the conflicts unintentional, and I do not think that the techniques of characterization are so simply divided: on the one hand, the "tragic" rhetoric of "emphatically colored and manipulated language" and, on the other hand, the detached portrayal of an adolescent. This distinction between rhetoric and realism obscures an important point, which critics continually overlook: much of that "heroic" rhetoric is actually mock-heroic; much of it is parody which should complicate our reactions

From *Nineteenth-Century Fiction* 25, no. 4 (March 1971).

to the intentionally elevating passages of the book. Once one explores Hardy's various uses of grand styles and of classical, mythical, and chivalric allusions, one begins to see that he is not merely trying to pass a silly dreamer off as a tragic heroine; he is using many literary resources to present a complex and conflicting view of romanticism. Furthermore, one discovers that Hardy is not using rhetoric arbitrarily to elevate or mock. I hope to show in this study that he establishes two sets of literary and cultural traditions in order to present his romantic heroine from two opposing points of view, to present her both as the tragic Queen of Night and as the comic and morbid courtly pretender.

From her first appearance in the novel it is clear that Eustacia must destroy herself or be destroyed by forces to which she will not submit, and throughout there are foreshadowings of her inevitably violent death: her brilliant but wasteful bonfire, her proud isolation, the associations with darkness and Hell, her vexing combination of stubbornness and impulsiveness, her grand schemes and dislike for a schemer's caution, her impossible dreams. But inevitable destruction, even self-destruction, is not necessarily tragic, since both character and action must be grand enough to call for a tragic response; and here we come to Hardy's conflicting attitudes toward his heroine. On the one hand, as she is the Promethean rebel and Queen of Night, he suggests by allusion, imagery, and direct statement that her longings are titanic, or at least demonic. Although he does not imply that such rebelliousness is socially or ethically desirable, he does show an aesthetic admiration for the willfulness and passion of this seductress. He elevates his tragic heroine by associating her with classical myth, the folklore of magic, and the most primitive, numenous aspects of nature. On the other hand, however, he also represents her as a vain, naive, arrogant daydreamer, a girl whose passion so exceeds her imagination and experience that she cannot conceive of adequate objects for her desire. From this point of view the content of her dreams appears literary, trite, and socially affected; even her passion seems at times to be not only escapist, but self-indulgently morbid. This satirical view of Eustacia also has a pattern of associations. To complement the mythic, magical, and primitive associations of the tragic heroine, Hardy relates his satirical character to themes and symbols of courtly traditions. By alluding to and at times parodying courtly love he can connect Eustacia's affectation, triteness, and morbidity; and he can establish two opposing literary and cultural frames of reference by which to judge his character either as the heroine of romantic tragedy or the *alazon* of a comedy satirizing romanticism.

Since the tragic pattern of associations has been elaborated in several discussions of the novel, it should be enough to summarize its main characteristics. First seen silhouetted atop the Celtic barrow and next represented by her explicitly Promethean fire, Eustacia is at once associated with pagan cultures far older than the quasi-Christian culture of most of the heath-dwellers. Rumored by several characters to be a witch, she is able to draw Damon Wildeve as her candle draws his signal moth, and her power over him is sometimes compared to that of a conjurer: in a clever play upon fairy tales she seems nearly capable of materializing him from a frog, and she herself likens that act to the Witch of Endor's calling up Samuel (bk. 1, chap. 6). She also has still closer affinities with the underworld, for the narrator claims that in her "true Tartarean dignity" she is trapped in a Hades of Egdon, a defiant goddess confined in a wasteland. By the time that she makes her last journey across the heath the continuously expanding allusions and analogues have made the scene nearly apocalyptic: "I was a night which led the traveller's thoughts instinctively to dwell on nocturnal scenes of disaster in the chronicles of the world, on all that is terrible and dark in history and legend—the last plague of Egypt, the destruction of Sennacherib's host, the agony in Gethsemane" (bk. 5, chap. 7). Of course, Hardy is occasionally ironic toward his paganism, as in his comic portrayals of the superstitious Christian Cantle and Susan Nunsuch, but even these lighter instances can help to reinforce the tragic pattern: as Susan melts the wax effigy of Eustacia, her victim is already nearing her death in the storm. Although Hardy remains skeptical toward the supernatural (as shown by Eustacia's and Thomasin's contrasting reactions to the heath [bk. 5, chap. 8]), he frequently uses it to heighten the tragic elements.

Eustacia's grand passions, however, are not always so impressively heightened; they become debased and even foolish when they are stylized into a decadent, clumsy imitation of courtly manners. When Wildeve comes to her on the heath to discuss his marrying Thomasin, her melancholy changes to petulant affectation as she scorns him for a violation of courtly love: "You have not valued my courtesy—the courtesy of a lady in loving you—who used to think of far more ambitious things" (bk. 1, chap. 9). She particularly resents having been defeated by a woman who represents marriage and respectability, the main opponents of the grand passion. She makes the connection between marriage and respectability quite explicit when she sneers, "Marry her—she is nearer to your own position in life than I am!" Ironically, Eustacia also envies social position, which is one of the reasons she marries Clym, but she cannot admit to such mundane longings; thus she takes some bitter comfort in thinking herself more sophisticated than the prosperous, but rather bourgeois, Yeobright women.

Earlier in the novel, Thomasin Yeobright, whom Wildeve describes as "such a confoundedly good little woman," unwittingly contrasts her bourgeois values with Eustacia's courtly code. Partly from fear of being socially shamed by a broken engagement, she humbles herself to Wildeve and says, "Here am I asking you to marry me, when by rights you ought to be on your knees imploring me, your cruel mistress, not to refuse you, and saying it should break your heart if I did" (book 1, chap. 5). Of course, Thomasin, who eventually will find her true love through a maypole dance and settle down on a dairy farm, does not really believe in such courtly "rights." To her the cruel mistress is no more than the pleasantly coy maiden who fully intends to maintain her purity and secure a husband. Her next statement reveals her attitude: "I used to think it would be pretty and sweet like that." Eustacia Vye would have little concern for this prettiness and sweetness, for she understands more fully the meaning of the cruel mistress to which her rival naively refers.

Eustacia understands it, however, in a vulgarized form appropriate to a sensual and, despite her pretenses, unsophisticated girl. Far from considering love a god to whom she must surrender her freedom in a quasi-religious devotion, she feels that lovers' constancy is as tedious as marriage. In fact, she not only shows the fickleness of some mistresses in Renaissance sonnets, she even insists that her lover ought to be unfaithful to her: "Love is the dismallest thing where the lover is quite honest." When she scorns Wildeve for his relations with Thomasin, she does not object to his infidelity; instead, she claims that his passions are inferior to hers and that he does not love either woman intensely enough. In such an attitude Eustacia is far from the values of the medieval traditions; she has more in common, in this respect, with the later Don Juan figures in the decadence of those traditions. Unable to find a lover commensurate with the "abstraction called passionate love," for which Hardy says she longs, she must be frustrated in a number of inadequate objects of her desire. And the frustration is a much vulgarized form of that experienced by the characters of medieval romances and courtly literature. As Denis de Rougemont has shown in detail, the ideal of passion requires that the love be thwarted so that the unconsummated desire can be prolonged for its own sake (*Love in the Western World,* bk. 1, chap. 7). Eustacia differs in two important respects. First, she sometimes implies that she herself is almost aware of the pattern, that she actually wants to be thwarted in love for the melancholic pleasure: "I should hate it all to be quite smooth. Indeed, I think I like you to desert me a little once now and then" (bk. 1, chap. 9). Second, she does not pine for a prohibited lover; she despairs because she cannot find one lover for whom she can pine. Although Clym momentarily fulfills the role, she pursues him, marries him, and converts her romantic symbol into a frustratingly real man. Consequently, instead of an Iseult or even a Guinevere we have a slightly ridiculous, lonely, bored young girl who would like to be a passionate, even a tragic, lover, but who must complain that her circumstances do not provide the opportunities. She has confounded literary myth and reality as completely as the self-deceiving heroines of Flaubert and Jane Austen.

When Hardy is describing her in terms of courtly love, he can be quite pointedly satiric. Rather than representing her as a burlesqued courtly lady, however, he uses an Ovidian tradition and presents her, ironically as the cruel and arbitrary mock-goddess. In doing so, he can underscore her inconstancy and parody her role as the tragic Promethean goddess. He first satirizes her in the terms of Ovidian irony in the famous Queen of Night chapter:

> Eustacia Vye was the raw material of a divinity. On Olympus she would have done well with a little preparation. She had the passions and instincts which make a model goddess, that is, those which make not quite a model woman. Had it been possible for the earth and mankind to be entirely in her grasp for a while, had she handled the distaff, the spindle, and the shears at her own free will, few in the world would have noticed the change of government. There would have been the same inequity of lot, the same heaping up of favours here, of contumely there, the same generosity before justice, the same perpetual dilemmas, the same captious alteration of caresses and blows that we endure now.
>
> (bk. 1, chap. 7)

Aside from any relation to themes of fate and chance which appear obtrusively throughout the novel, this description has its satiric force mainly in conventional parody. I am puzzled that so many commentators have used this "Queen of Night" chapter—and in particular this quoted passage—to pont out that Hardy romantically deifies Eustacia and yet have not noticed how ironic he sometimes is toward this apotheosis. Albert Guerard points out that this chapter "employs all the rhetorical devices of Pater's famous meditation on the Gioconda," and he finds it surprising that Eustacia does survive "such a grandiloquent introduction." Walter Allen claims that "there is no implied criticism of her attitudes" and that "all Hardy's powers of evocation are showered upon her": then, to illustrate his points, he quotes the passage which I have quoted above (*The English Novel*). Robert Evans claims that "by a tour de force in chapter seven [Hardy] creates a Eustacia eminently fitted to this tragic world" and cites supporting descriptions, some of which seem heavily ironic. The trouble comes from Hardy's ambivalence. There is much of Pater's impressionism in the chapter, and there is a forceful, at times forced, attempt to give Eustacia a "Tartarean dignity." But there is also mockery of that attempt—not just because the literal Eustacia cannot entirely support such dignity, but also because Hardy cannot take such dark goddesses completely seriously, cannot help seeing some pompousness in the elevation. Is Hardy completely serious, let alone solemn and tragic, when he describes Eustacia as "the raw material of a divinity," as though goddesses were manufactured out of human "raw material"? And what of the tone of the next two sentences? What kind of "little preparation" makes one "do well" on Olympus, and what is a "model goddess"—something like a model wife or a model husband? If Hardy is trying here to create a Gioconda, he is slighting his images, diction, and tone. Even about the rest of the passage one cannot say for sure that Hardy is not being somewhat arch, especially since it describes Eustacia in one of her own favorite roles, as a cruel, whimsical arbiter of man's fate.

As the chapter continues, Hardy remains ambivalent toward her, vacillating in tone between awe and wit, and he often represents the conflicting attitudes through an opposition of the two metaphorical patterns: there is the potentially tragic Eustacia of "pagan eyes, full of nocturnal mysteries," and the comic Eustacia of "celestial imperiousness, love, wrath, and fervour [which] had proved to be somewhat thrown away on netherward Egdon." There is the queen of solitude whose proper setting is the Rainbarrow and the affected queen of love who will soon say quite ludicrously of Thomasin, "She has come between me and my inclination."

This ambivalence continues throughout the novel, sometimes making it impossible for one to react simply to Eustacia's comments and actions. Consider, for example, her complaint to Wildeve, "But do I desire unreasonably much in wanting what is called life—music, poetry, passion, war, and all the beating and pulsing that are going on in the great arteries of the world?" (bk. 4, chap. 6). Here is the passionate, restless woman, whose vitality is suggested by her imagery of pulsing arteries. But here also is the comically pretentious woman who knows the chivalric formula for "what is called life—music, poetry, passion, war." If she has known little suitable music and poetry, she has known even less war. Her ideals are derived and fanciful, and they suggest the fundamental connection of love and war found throughout courtly literature (compare de Rougemont, bk. 5). Accordingly, her "high gods" are William the Conqueror, Strafford, Napoleon, Saul, Sisera, and Pontius Pilate. But all the wars that Eustacia can enjoy are a few local skirmishes against Mrs. Yeobright.

In order to decide why Hardy uses such courtly parody, one must move beyond literary analysis and speculate about his attitudes toward romantic aspiration. In part, this satire may reflect Hardy's feeling that the Gioconda and the Promethean heroine are stunted in a century that can no longer offer adequate ends for their passion. This corresponds to a common social theme in his major novels: Michael Henchard becomes an anachronistic patriarch in a society that is substituting bookkeeping and farm machinery for personal strength; the aristocratic d'Urbervilles have been replaced by the bourgeois Stoke-d'Urbervilles; and Jude Fawley's dream of the intellectual life greatly exceeds the reality of that life presented in the novel. As the possibilities for grand actions decrease, the passion leads to increasingly clumsy gestures. Secondly, perhaps Hardy is also considering the corruption of passion by class consciousness: the seductress as social snob. This possibility is reinforced by the extent of class concern in the later novels and particularly by the character of Lucetta in *The Mayor of Casterbridge*. Although a far less powerful character than Eustacia, Lucetta is also the dark, adulterous, European seductress; and she, too, is particularly defensive about her origins and vain about her social position. Finally, and perhaps most importantly, Hardy seems to be showing ambivalent feelings toward all romantic aspiration. The problem, then, would lie not only in the historical and social contexts that corrupt heroic passion but in the ambiguities of the basic passions themselves. To put Eustacia into flattering literary company for a moment, she has much in common with Milton's Satan, if one considers the whole of *Paradise Lost*. Both rebels have awesome energy, independence, limitless desire, and a stubborn courage to resist their circumstances; in this sense, whether he knew it or not, Hardy was of Eustacia's party. But both rebels are also fanatically arrogant, petty, comic egotists; and they have to be so, given their authors' views of the romantic rebellion against reality. If this speculation about Hardy's intention is valid, we can see why he has not merely given us either a tragic Promethean heroine or a comic-pathetic Emma Bovary. He has given us, instead, a double perspective on the romantic heroine; he has shown her tremendous energies and ridiculous self-delusions. And he has done it well. He has not just dressed an adolescent girl in some rhetorical ornaments, a Madame Bovary in buskins. He has presented a character who is variously a heroine and the parody of a heroine, a Queen of Night and a courtly pretender, or *alazon,* who must be ridiculed by mock-heroic techniques.

This romantic heroine is both a goddess and a mortal walking on stilts, playing at divinity. Thus, Hardy uses two complementary sets of metaphors to describe the double nature of such heroism: the tragic metaphors of classical myth and folklore and the satiric or mock-heroic metaphors of a debased and bungled courtly love.

Hardy does not always use courtly love themes for comic parody, however. He also uses them to criticize the romantic heroine in more somber and more deeply psychological ways in order to show that her aspirations are not only foolish at times but almost diseased at others. He realizes that this "abstraction called passionate love" is fundamentally morbid. Whereas the tragic pattern must inevitably result in death as a consequence of Promethean rebellion, the courtly pattern reveals the search for death. Death consummates the romantic quest for an experience that transmutes what Eustacia considers the banality of her life. As de Rougemont has claimed, by the late nineteenth century the myth of fatal passion had become so democratized that its underlying impulses became fully explicit (bk. 4, chaps. 18–21). Eustacia, as well as the narrator, seems to realize at times that her longings cannot be satisfied in life, not even by Budmouth or Paris. In her last speech in the novel her protest is absolute, encompassing far more than her immediate circumstances: "O, the cruelty of putting me into this ill-conceived world" (bk. 5, chap. 7). Eustacia's morbidity is fundamentally different from the self-destructiveness that has often been noted in other of Hardy's characters. Clym Yeobright, Michael Henchard, and Tess Durbeyfield have all been interpreted as self-destructive, even as showing persistent death-wishes; but the partial causes of those impulses are guilt, curses, and even—in the case of Clym—what Hardy will come to call "the ache of modernism." By the time of *Jude the Obscure* Hardy goes so far as to write of the will not to live. But Eustacia's desires do not stem from guilt or modernism. She does not desire not to live; she wants to die, for she is at least half in love with easeful death. Thus her dreams become suffused with death as a form of an intensely passionate experience.

Two of the most clearly symbolic scenes that originate in her passion for the once-Parisian Clym closely associate love, death, and chivalry. In the dream which comes shortly after she has seen Clym out walking she dances with a silver-armored knight, dives with him into a pool on the heath, emerges into an "iridescent hollow, arched with rainbows," and sees him fall into fragments as he is about to remove his visored helmet to kiss her (bk. 2, chap. 3). Except for a reversal of the usual male and female roles (for which there is some precedent), the dream follows closely an archetypal pattern of passionate transcendence: the unknown lover from beyond this world, the symbolic drowning, the rebirth into a beautiful, isolated grotto, and the mysterious disappearance of the lover. Medieval literature has many similar representations of the earthly paradise or underworld, e.g. the Celtic hollow hill and Under-the-Wave-Land and the Old Norse hollow mountain. Frequently these medieval paradises are associated with love, often with the seduction of a knight by a fay, including the particularly relevant Dame du Lac and even Venus, who entertained Tannhäuser in her paradisal cave. Occasionally the sexual roles are reversed, with the seducer being a mysterious knight of the Lake, as in the French lay *Tydorel* and the English ballad of Lady Isabel and the Elf Knight. In the twelfth and thirteenth centuries these motifs from Arthurian romance were blended with French courtly traditions, and later versions usually descend from the double source. Two of the most obvious examples of the cave-love-death associations in the nineteenth century are Keats's "La Belle Dame Sans Merci," with its faint courtly suggestions in the fairy child's name, and cantos 2–4 of Byron's *Don Juan*, in which the hero is cast into the sea to be healed in a cave by a beautiful mistress of natural nobility. The extent to which Hardy relies on such traditions seems obvious in the completeness of his pattern, even to the use of "wonderous music," "ecstatic" mazes of the dance, and Eustacia's feeling "like a woman in Paradise." And one hardly need apply modern psychology to find the erotic morbidity of her dream: this combination of fairy lore and courtly love has that meaning within its traditions, and Hardy makes sure that the reader will not miss the pointed symbolism: "It had as many ramifications as the Cretan labyrinth."

The second of these two symbolic scenes is the mummers' play in which Eustacia, trying to gain entrance to Clym's house, plays the Turk who is slain by St. George. Although the play originated in a vegetative rite of Summer's overcoming Winter, which has significance for the seasonal myths in the novel, it has been converted into a chivalric form, as the legendary St. George was converted in the twelfth and thirteenth centuries into the patron of chivalry and protector of the crusaders. So, appropriately, Eustacia's romance with Clym begins with her being killed by the Christian knight who had performed the central romantic quest of killing the dragon to rescue the King's daughter.

In view of the double pattern of tragic myth and fatal courtly love it is appropriate that Hardy leaves Eustacia's death ambiguous. We do not know whether the mythic heroine is destroyed by a Nature that she defied or the courtly lover commits suicide in a desperate surrender to the silver-armored knight of romance and death. The body floating in the dark winter pool resolves both movements, even though they are as different as a terrible hubris and a self-indulgent pathos. Just as Hardy balances his tragic conception of Eustacia with a comic parody, so he also balances it with a representation of a fatal and decadent passion. Again the double conception suggests his ambivalence toward romantic heroism, perhaps because he realizes that that hero is rebelling not only against his restricting circumstances but against life itself.

Thus, I would suggest that Hardy is not really confused in his conflicting representations of Eustacia; he is purposeful and even systematic at times. One could still legitimately object that Eustacia is too much manipulated by the author's attitudes to be a coherently realistic character. And one could legitimately claim that this novel is not generically pure, either as a tragedy or a satire. But these familiar objections are too concerned with what the book is not, and not enough with what it is. I have tried to show that, at least in one important aspect, it is a complex ordering of Hardy's attitudes toward romanticism and that it achieves that order largely by presenting Eustacia through two sets of opposed literary traditions which show her to be both a tragic Queen of Night and a comic and morbid courtly pretender.

The Return of the Repressed

Perry Meisel

The apparently Darwinian asides in Knight's cliff adventure [in *A Pair of Blue Eyes*] and at moments in *Far from the Madding Crowd* seemed designed to give expression to a scientific view of nature, assigning an external determinism to a universe that encompasses both the individual and the community. But, as we have seen in Darwin, such a view simply upholds the illusions of a myopic rationalism that refuses to examine its own perceiving lens. By the time he wrote *The Return of the Native,* Hardy seems to have been forced to tackle the initial conflict—between intellect and desire, rational, urban individual and rural community—by reassessing his entire imaginative perspective. The journey into the self has begun: the lens itself must be scrutinized. The question of method becomes correspondingly problematic as the irony of the book, that a native of Wessex has become the rationalist, suggests the involution that is underway.

If we are to believe Albert Guerard's remark that in "every novel we stumble unexpectedly upon signs of the struggle of an undigested idea, an undramatized contrast, an unconcealed and grossly abstract intention . . . [and that] the novels must transcend their theoretical conceptions before they can hope to interest us," then we must ignore the importance of that very struggle. For, in his early attempts at fiction, Hardy brought the individual intellect to bear on the community, and, sensing difficulties, moved to examine both the nature of community and of the individual. We have seen the implications of the kind of rationalism embraced by Leslie

From *Thomas Hardy: The Return of the Repressed: A Study of the Major Fiction.*

Stephen; Hardy, as an artist who was tremendously drawn to rational modes of thought, must have felt the need to search beyond the intellect. And while it seems that he retained a conscious belief in the faculty of reason (even if it led only to despair), his imagination was still free to move elsewhere. Yet the deeper he drove to the recesses of his characters, tracing the minute details of their inner lives in an attempt to resolve the conflict, the more his rational propensities rebelled at being sentenced to silence. His "churchiness," or sense of community, had been destroyed by Knight just as his religious orthodoxy had been reduced to ruins.

At about the time *The Return of the Native* was completed, Hardy recorded two reflections that begin to suggest the outline of this maturer period:

> April-Note. A Plot, or Tragedy, should arise from the gradual closing in of a situation that comes of ordinary human passions, prejudices, and ambitions, by reason of the characters taking no trouble to ward off the disastrous events produced by the said passions, prejudices, and ambitions.
>
> The advantages of the letter-system of telling a story (passing over the disadvantages) are that, hearing what one side has to say, you are led constantly to the imagination of what the other side must be feeling, and at last are anxious to know if the other side does really feel what you imagine.

Here, he places responsibility directly with his characters, invoking no determinism from without—the implication is, instead, that whatever determinants exist within a narrative are "by reason of the characters [themselves] taking no trouble to ward off the disastrous events produced"; what happens to them is a function of their own constitutions. By the "advantages of the letter-system" of storytelling, he seems to reaffirm our understanding of the poetics of the early novels: that the world of a novel becomes alive only when events become important to the characters and, as a result, affect the community in which they move.

An entry of the same month rounds out Hardy's intellectual recognition of the growing dramatic processes now refining the modes already followed in his earlier work:

> April 22. The method of Boldini, the painter of "The Morning Walk" in the French Gallery two or three years ago . . . —of Hobbema, in his view of a road with formal lopped trees and flat tame scenery—is that of infusing emotion into the baldest

> external objects either by the presence of a human figure among them, or by mark of some human connection with them.
>
> This accords with my feeling about, say, Heidelberg and Baden *versus* Scheveningen—as I wrote at the beginning of *The Return of the Native*—that the beauty of association is entirely superior to the beauty of aspect, and a beloved relative's old battered tankard to the finest Greek vase. Paradoxically put, it is to see the beauty in ugliness.

His concern with the relation between landscape and the human figure assumes a form which reveals the needs that have wrought refinements in his poetics. The meaning of his earlier remark now becomes even more significant: "The writer's problem is, how to strike a balance between the uncommon and the ordinary . . . [while] . . . human nature must never be made abnormal. . . . The uncommonness must be in the events, not in the characters." At the same time, "[t]ragedy . . . should arise from the gradual closing in of a situation that comes of ordinary human passions" and ordinary human weaknesses in response to those passions. But Hardy stresses, too, that the "poetry of a scene varies with the minds of the perceivers." Thus landscape, in the sense of the relation between external scenery or objects and human figures, becomes the most natural mode for mediating the demands of his poetics. The "beauty of association" can be used as a means of defining character and event from a character's perspective. Even with some intellectual awareness of these possibilities, though, Hardy still uses landscape in only a limited way at this point in his career: as a reflection, by simile or analogy, of his characters' moods and natures. As his substantive concerns move away from a community-oriented perspective (where individuals are seen in terms of a society, as either members or intruders) toward the perspective of the individual himself, his imaginative methods become correspondingly refined. Hardy's changing use of landscape is important both as a mediator between human community and nature and as a means of creating individual consciousness. *The Return of the Native* furnishes the richest example of this brooding transitional period, as the universe of the early novels moves toward the vision of the later Hardy.

The opening chapter of the novel turns on the suspended transition from day to night on Egdon Heath. It is the counterpart in external, inanimate nature to the suspended moments between waking and sleeping in individual consciousness described in the opening chapter of Proust's *Remembrance of Things Past*. The comparison is strikingly suggestive of a direction Hardy was just beginning to pursue at the time he wrote *The Return of the Native*. In a book that appeared the year before the first volume of Proust's work, Freud's *Totem and Taboo* (1912), the significance of our comparison finds apt conceptual expression: "owing to the projection outwards of internal perceptions, primitive men arrived at a picture of the external world which we, with our intensified conscious perception, have now to translate back into psychology." "We are thus prepared to find that primitive man transposed the structural conditions of his own mind into the external world; and we may attempt to reverse the process and put back into the human mind what animism teaches as to the nature of things."

> In fact, precisely at this transitional point of its nightly roll into darkness the great and particular glory of the Egdon waste began, and nobody could be said to understand the heath who had not been there at such a time. It could best be felt when it could not clearly be seen . . . then, and only then, did it tell its true tale . . . the sombre stretch of rounds and hollows seemed to rise and meet the evening gloom in pure sympathy, the heath exhaling darkness as rapidly as the heavens precipitated it. And so the obscurity in the air and the obsurity in the land closed together in a black fraternization toward which each advanced halfway.
>
> The place became full of a watchful intentness now; for when other things sank brooding to sleep the heath appeared slowly to awake and listen. Every night its Titanic form seemed to await something; but it had waited thus, unmoved, during so many centuries, through the crises of so many things, that it could only be imagined to await one last crisis—the final overthrow.

> For a long time I used to go to bed early. Sometimes, when I had put out my candle, my eyes would close so quickly that I had not even time to say "I'm going to sleep." And half an hour later the thought that it was time to go to sleep would awaken me. . . . [An] impression would persist for some moments after I was awake; it did not disturb my mind, but it lay like scales upon my eyes and prevented them from registering the fact that the candle was no longer burning. Then it would begin to seem unintelligible, as the thoughts of a former existence must be to a reincarnate spirit.
>
> When a man is asleep, he has in a circle round him the chain

of the hours, the sequence of the years, the order of the heavenly host. Instinctively, when he awakes, he looks to these, and in an instant reads off his own position on the earth's surface and the amount of time that has elapsed during his slumbers; but this ordered procession is apt to grow confused and to break its ranks.

(Marcel Proust, *Swann's Way*)

In *The Return of the Native,* Hardy's landscape becomes personalized to a much greater degree than at any point in his earlier novels. And, as if to substantiate the feeling that the heath itself represents the explicit description of the psyche Proust was to achieve, the artist tells us that "[h]aggard Egdon appealed to a subtler and scarcer instinct, to a more recently learnt emotion, than that which responds to the sort of beauty called charming and fair." The separation between the perceiver and scene, of course, still remains; but an affinity between the perceptive sensibility and the nature of the world it beholds is clearly suggested. Hardy's early diary entry has already suggested this tendency: "The poetry of a scene varies with the minds of the perceivers. Indeed, it does not lie in the scene at all"; "the beauty of association" that he notes at the time of his completion of the novel confirms the fact that he was also moving consciously in this direction. The passage in the novel to which he refers in the note takes on added meaning in the context of the landscape:

> Human souls may find themselves in closer and closer harmony with external things wearing a somberness distasteful to our race when it was young. The time seems near, if it has not actually arrived, when the chastened sublimity of a moor, a sea, or a mountain, will be all of nature that is absolutely in keeping with the moods of the more thinking among mankind. And ultimately, to the commonest tourist, spots like Iceland may become what the vineyards and myrtle-gardens of South Europe are to him now; and Heidelberg and Baden be passed unheeded as he hastens from the Alps to the sand-dunes of Scheveningen.

As Egdon takes on symbolic proportions, he moves further:

> Intensity was more usually reached by way of the brilliant, and such a sort of intensity was often arrived at during winter darkness, tempests, and mists. Then Egdon was aroused to reciprocity; for the storm was its lover and the wind its friend. Then it became the home of strange phantoms; *and it was found to be*

> *the hitherto unrecognized original of those wild regions of obscurity which are vaguely felt to be compassing us about in midnight dreams of flight and disaster, and are never thought of after the dream till revived by scenes like this.* [My italics.]

The aspect of the heath in Hardy's imagination becomes "the hitherto unrecognized *original* of those wild regions of obscurity" glimpsed in our most terrible dreams. It is the bedrock of man's essence, but the tension inherent in his imagination holds the language to analogy, just short of identity:

> It was at present a place perfectly accordant with man's nature—neither ghastly, hateful, nor ugly; neither commonplace, unmeaning, nor tame; but, like man, slighted and enduring; and withal singularly colossal and mysterious in its swarthy monotony. . . . It had a lonely face, suggesting tragical possibilities. The untameable, Ishmaelitish thing that Egdon now was it always had been. Civilization was its enemy.

But momentarily he is set free to describe the deepest stratum of the scene in its resemblance to man's nature (the topographical language is strangely akin to Freud's images of the psyche):

> To recline on a stump of thorn in the central valley of Egdon, between afternoon and night, as now, where the eye could reach nothing of the world outside the summits and shoulders of heathland which filled the whole circumference of its glance, and to know that everything around and underneath had been from prehistoric times as unaltered as the stars overhead, gave ballast to the mind adrift on change, and harassed by the irrepressible New. The great inviolate place had an ancient permanence which the sea cannot claim.

Here lies the realm of instinct, that which alone remains natural in man—"the hitherto unrecognized original." An implicit contrast is made in the passage between the central valley, suggesting the unconscious id whose peaks and crags prohibit converse with the demands of the external world, and the conscious mind, a faculty distinct from this valley, "adrift on change," "harassed by the irrepressible New," which must come to recognize that the central valley is its true home.

As the chapter closes, the suspended vision is brought into relation with the external world. Hardy discloses the existence of "an aged highway," the only aspect of the landscape that marks man's conscious intentions within the wilderness. Before a human figure appears on the scene, then, the artist has established a new fictional universe. It is a world where both the impulses of the conscious individual and the community are allowed expression. Unlike *A Pair of Blue Eyes,* where Knight predominates because of the rawness of his fresh discovery, and *Far from the Madding Crowd,* where that impulse was suppressed with the result of an infected community, Hardy is now ready to confront the struggle between the two worlds as he builds upon a new foundation.

Just as the first chapter of *The Return of the Native* establishes a psychological landscape against which the action of the novel takes place, the first book of the novel, "The Three Women," forms a prologue to the real plot, which does not really begin until Clym appears in the second book. It announces the capacities of man (conscious, acting man) within the limits of mortal existence: a rumbling underworld of dark passion, "the central valley," weighing against humanity from below, and an equally unknown and threatening world without, including "Civilization . . . its enemy." While at first the landscape of the opening chapter seems only static, its dynamic nature is revealed in that "black fraternization" of sky and earth, light and dark. The first chapter is a metaphor for the human mind; within it, or against it, Hardy's characters play out their lives.

As if the presence of tension were not perceptible already, the title of the second chapter states the obvious: "Humanity Appears on the Scene Hand in Hand with Trouble." The landscape now changes from symbol to reality, as the first human figure, old Captian Vye, makes his way along the road through the wilderness. As soon as Hardy describes him we see yet another human figure on the road, but this time from the first character's point of view. Thus, in two strokes, Hardy moves, first, from a symbolic overview to a more realistic mode, and then directly into the world of men. But the impression of the first chapter remains; the human world has been infused with the atmosphere of the opening pages on Egdon, as we see Venn through Vye's eyes: "It was the single atom of life that the scene contained, and it only served to render the general loneliness more evident." That Hardy grants the perceiving eye to a single character (if only for one sentence) testifies to the meaning of the movement of these first pages.

At this transitional hour "there was that in the condition of the heath itself which resembled protracted halting and dubiousness," a condition betraying the tension of the dynamic elements that have been suggested so far. Mystery and intrigue have already figured in the action, too—the woman in Venn's van, the presence of the reddleman himself, and Eustacia's form upon the hill. When the rustics group at the spot abandoned by Eustacia, we learn that she "had no relation to the forms who had taken her place." There is irony and a leaden foreshadowing in Hardy's formalized response to her departure:

> The imagination of the observer clung by preference to that vanished, solitary figure, as to something more interesting, more important, more likely to have a history worth knowing than these new-comers, and unconsciously regarded them as intruders.

Hardy betrays his sympathies early—Eustacia is the intruder upon the heath, the danger to the community; but we already feel that the forces of nature are in secret alliance with her. The barrenness of the soil on the heath exposes the community: we can see the true outlines of society more easily here than in the richer agricultural areas of Wessex. With the bonfires ablaze, the community functions at its most primitive level to the discerning spiritual eye:

> In the heath's barrenness to the farmer lay its fertility to the historian. There had been no obliteration because there had been no tending.
>
> It was as if the bonfire-makers were standing in some radiant upper story of the world, detached from and independent of the dark stretches below. The heath down there was now a vast abyss, and no longer a continuation of what they stood on; for their eyes, adapted to the blaze, could see nothing of the deeps beyond its influence.

With this view comes a response:

> Moreover, to light a fire is the instinctive and resistant act of man when, at the winter ingress, the curfew is sounded throughout Nature. It indicates a spontaneous, Promethean rebelliousness against the fiat that this recurrent season shall bring foul time, cold darkness, misery and death. Black chaos comes, and the fettered gods of the earth say, Let there be light.

And since the poetry of a scene issues from the nature of its perception, Hardy recalls the stark outlines:

> Those whom Nature had depicted as merely quaint became grotesque, the grotesque became preternatural; for all was in extremity.

This is November on the heath, when the land betrays its starkest qualities and man is called upon to preserve the species; it seems that Hardy sees winter as the truest expression of the heath since in its barrenness "lay its fertility to the historian." Man's Promethean rebelliousness at this symbolic fire-time reveals not his conquest of nature, but his blindness to "the dark stretches below," the mental accompaniment to this material need for warmth. Fire is civilization, "Civilization [Egdon's] enemy": the perverse Platonic overtones in the inhabitants' adaptation to the ironic and reverse truth of their fires evoke a seething picture of the dynamics of human society and nature. Paradoxically, in answering his needs man blinds himself to his own nature (given the dual function of the heath as a symbol of man's unconscious and as actual physical nature). The potential for the destruction of the community no longer lies with an external interference; it is latent within the society itself. The seeds of its destruction lurk within its blindness to its own nature.

The community, however, can remain stable as long as it huddles by its fires, ignorant of "the dark stretches below." In an article on the Dorsetshire laborer in *Longman's Magazine* in July 1883, Hardy was to write:

> It is among such communities as these that happiness will find her last refuge upon earth, since it is among them that a perfect insight into the conditions of existence will be longest postponed.

The potential threat to order, however, lies in the possibility of a consciousness of the true power of "the vast abyss below." Such a consciousness may be evoked by a perspective that is not bound to the community. While an intrusive intelligence was seen as the cause of infection in the early novels, it now becomes only the catalyst for self-recognition, "the mind adrift on change." The "irrepressible New" can only be awareness of "the hitherto unrecognized original." This is the point from which a formulation of Hardy's sense of "modern" must begin: the extension of consciousness from the deceptive light of the most newly built fire to the surrounding territories of darkness.

But a conflict lies at the very heart of the discovery: *all* fires must be extinguished in order to learn to see in the darkness. The state of suspension between the extinction of the fires and the ability to move in the night is the ground of the struggle; it is the abyss into which Hardy's major characters must now descend. Their journeys and their fates, once they confront "the hitherto unrecognized," comprise tragedy. With Hardy's next major work, *The Mayor of Casterbridge,* we shall see a full statement of this kind of tragedy—"modern" tragedy—when the confrontation occurs within the mind (the wish as deed) without the necessity of acting. But because the artist himself is groping in the darkness, Henchard's tragedy must still be *communicated* to us primarily by his actions, while the dynamics of the tragic individual himself, as we shall see, are internal. In spite of the suggestive opening of *The Return of the Native,* the novel holds back from fulfilling itself in this direction, and we must wait for *The Mayor* to see the fuller design.

Hardy focuses more closely on Eustacia in the first book than on any other character. She returns to the barrow after the rustics have departed: "There she stood still, around her stretching the vast night atmosphere, whose incomplete darkness in comparison with the total darkness of the heath below it might have represented a venial beside a mortal sin." In spite of her hatred of the heath and of her situation, it seems that Eustacia is at one with the symbolic proportions of the landscape. As if to confirm a suggested analogy, Hardy has told us that "[p]ersons with any weight of character carry, like planets, their atmospheres along with them in their orbits." Because Eustacia is an outsider by temperament as well as by history, we sense an irony in the remark that "the observer clung by preference to [her] vanished, solitary figure" on the hill, and "unconsciously regarded [the rustics themselves] as outsiders." What Guerard calls "the progressive domination of nature by temperament" in the development of the novels ("The poetry of a scene varies with the minds of the perceivers") describes both the artist's consciousness and the possibilities of Eustacia's: precisely because her consciousness is predisposed to recognize "the hitherto unrecognized original," she is the catalyst for the possibility of the community's infection. "Such views of life were to some extent the natural begettings of her situation upon her nature." Through Clym, she will infect the community in that she will force it to realize the possibility of its destruction from within. The actual germ of the downfall of the old order is latent within the community itself—it becomes active when an exterior consciousness calls it into movement.

For Eustacia, her "woman's brain had authorized what it could not regulate"; her sighs are "but another phrase of the same discourse" as the winds. In her confrontation with her first lover, Wildeve, she speaks of "a strange warring [that] takes place in [her] mind." Her consciousness of her own microcosmic struggle is enriched by Hardy's loaded metaphors: "Whenever a flash of reason darted like an electric light upon her lover—as it sometimes would—and showed his imperfections, she shivered. . . . But it was over in a second, and she loved on." The definitive modern intellectual tool, "reason," and its symbolic product, "an electric light," bespeak her own "bonfire." Because she is ever willing to abandon its light, her choice is clear. She is likened to a pagan goddess:

> But celestial imperiousness, love, wrath, and fervour had proved to be somewhat thrown away on netherward Egdon. Her power was limited, and the consciousness of this limitation had biased her development. Egdon was her Hades, and since coming there she had imbibed much of what was dark in its tone, though inwardly and eternally unreconciled thereto.

The native inhabitants fear that she is a witch precisely because she poses a danger to the community. Just as "all was extremity" on the heath early in the book, there is "no middle distance in her perspective" either:

> Eustacia had got beyond the vision of some marriage of inexpressible glory; yet, though her emotions were in full vigour, she cared for no meaner union. Thus we see her in a strange state of isolation. To have lost the godlike conceit that we may do what we will, and not to have acquired a homely zest for doing what we can, shows a grandeur of temper which cannot be objected to in the abstract, for it denotes a mind that, though disappointed, forswears compromise. But, if congenial to philosophy, it is apt to be dangerous to the commonwealth. In a world where doing means marrying, and the commonwealth is one of hearts and hands, the same peril attends the condition.
>
> As far as social ethics were concerned, Eustacia approached the savage state, though in emotion she was all the while an epicure. She had advanced to the secret recesses of sensuousness, yet had hardly crossed the threshold of conventionality.

Eustacia's key position in the plot is now clear: she acts, of course, within the limits which have just been defined in her character and which correspond to the contours of the landscape early in the novel. That "strange warring" in her mind is a reflection of Egdon at twilight; that "black fraternization" suspends her between a refusal to use light and an equal refusal to explore the darkness. She is not quite a tragic character herself: but, given her relationship with Clym, she may throw the community, through him, into the abyss. Her refusals become her choices because of that forswearing of compromise, which, "if congenial to philosophy, . . . is apt to be dangerous to the commonwealth." She will not act upon her knowledge of the world within ("the secret recesses" to which she has advanced) and, thus, "had hardly crossed the threshold of conventionality"—but the visitation of that knowledge works upon all who come into contact with her. She has seen "the irrepressible New," but will not, or cannot, recognize it in herself. She feels the struggle within, but responds consciously only to her known, superficial desires.

Clym and Eustacia represent the two new ways in which Hardy tries to deal with his imaginative impulses in *The Return of the Native*. The lovers are both Knight's heirs: they combine his two most dangerous qualities, an intrusion into the community and a rational intelligence. But, having gone beyond the frontier of reason, Hardy has discovered a new counterpart to the inquiring (and now idealized) intellect, an alliance between natural forces and the passions of a woman. Where in the early novels, the individual's reason and the emotional bonds of the community formed the tension, the conflict has now shifted to a deeper level. With the infection of the community by reason, Hardy has begun to search for the limits of the reasoning capacity itself: Eustacia informs Clym, and both inform the dissolution of the strength of the ordered society.

After the wild, poetic strains of his descriptions of the heath and of Eustacia in the first book of the novel, Hardy's introduction of Yeobright allows the real action to begin. The strength of the lovers' union is defined in a perfect symbolic paradox that reveals the unity of the novel: "Take all the varying hates felt by Eustacia Vye towards the heath, and translate them into loves, and you have the heart of Clym." While the statement is definitive, it betrays Hardy's not infrequent reliance on a formula-like manner of conceptualization or summary. But in the very betrayal of such stylistic weaknesses, one of the central tensions in the imaginative universe is revealed. Indeed, the stylistic differences between Hardy's poetic language in describing the heath and Eustacia, and his leaden, conceptual, prosaic rendering of Clym, both express the artist's varying sympathies with his characters and the translation of that tension into other dualities issuing from the same source. Consider these descriptions of Clym against the earlier portraits of Eustacia:

> To one of middle age the countenance was that of a young man, though a youth might hardly have seen any necessity for the term of immaturity. But it was really one of those faces which convey less the idea of so many years as its age than of so much experience as its store. The number of their years may have been adequately summed up Jared, Mahalaleel, and the rest of the

> antediluvians, but the age of a modern man is to be measured by the intensity of his history.
>
> The face was well shaped, even excellently. But the mind within was beginning to use it as a mere waste tablet whereon to trace its idiosyncrasies as they developed themselves. The beauty here visible would in no long time be ruthlessly overrun by its parasite, thought.

> He already showed that thought is a disease of flesh, and indirectly bore evidence that ideal physical beauty is incompatible with emotional development and a full recognition of the coil of things. Mental luminousness must be fed with the oil of life, even though there is already a physical need for it; and the pitiful sight of two demands on one supply was just showing itself here.
>
> As for his look, it was a natural cheerfulness striving against depression from without, and not quite succeeding. The look suggested isolation, but revealed something more. As is usual with bright natures, the deity that lies ignominiously chained within an ephemeral human carcass shone out of him like a ray.
>
> The effect upon Eustacia was palpable.

Hardy's poetic rendering of Eustacia and prosaic presentation of Clym are complemental in terms of the view they grant us of the creating mind behind the fiction. Style becomes meaning and structure betrays content: Hardy as artist sympathizes with Eustacia and, even more, with the narrative consciousness he exhibits in the opening pages of the novel; on the other hand, the sympathies of Hardy the conceptualist and rational thinker lie with Clym and with his account of Yeobright's intellectual aspect. He has already called him "a modern man" whose age "is to be measured by the intensity of his history," like the heath's. It is precisely Clym's intellectual awareness of what Eustacia feels but cannot recognize that signifies his intellectual "modernism":

> He was a John the Baptist who took ennoblement rather than repentance for his text. Mentally he was in a provincial future, that is, he was in many points abreast with the central town thinkers of his date. Much of this development he may have owed to his studious life in Paris, where he had become acquainted with ethical systems popular at this time.
>
> In consequence of this relatively advanced position, Yeobright

> might have been called unfortunate. The rural world was not ripe for him.

But here the conflicting tendencies within Hardy's own mind appear in their reflection in the imaginative universe: the rural world of Egdon Heath, "away from comparisons," contains all that the most advanced conceptual minds of the age following Hardy's could recognize. It is his *dramatic* consciousness that approximates the next generation's concepts, both in the scenes of the heath and of Eustacia. But with his introduction of Clym, the idealized intellectual, Hardy's own efforts at thought (which, as an artist, he has condemned as "a disease of flesh") seem to take precedence over his dramatic impulses. Indeed, Hardy himself describes precisely this tension in an aside during one of his descriptions of Clym:

> When standing before certain men the philosopher regrets that thinkers are but perishable tissue, the artist that perishable tissue has to think. Thus to deplore, each from his point of view, the mutually destructive interdependence of spirit and flesh would have been instinctive with these in critically observing Yeobright.

And so it is the case with Hardy himself. Following his account of Clym's urbane "modernism," he writes:

> If anyone knew the heath well, it was Clym. He was permeated with its scenes, with its substance, and with its odours. He might be said to be its product. His eyes had first opened thereon; with its appearance all the first images of his memory were mingled.

As the model of the juxtaposition, then: "Much of [his intellectual] development *he may have owed to* his studious life in Paris, where he had become acquainted with the ethical systems popular at the time"; while "*He might be said to be* its [the heath's] product" (my italics). Hardy goes far in his attempt to dramatize Clym's harmony with his native home, especially in his role as furze-cutter, when even his mother cannot distinguish him from the landscape ("He was a brown spot in the midst of an expanse of olive-green gorse, and nothing more"; and, when his mother sees him, he "appeared as a mere parasite of the heath"). That Hardy uses the metaphor *parasite* as a description both of thought and of Clym's work upon the heath evidences the degree to which Clym's characterization touches upon central conflicts in the artist's imagination. The creation of Yeobright seems strained, almost artificial—especially in contrast to the flowing, breathing Eustacia.

The rustics exhibit distrust toward Clym, in spite of their long affection for him, when he reveals his plans to establish a school on the heath. He stirs essentially the same fear in the natives that prompts their condemnation of Eustacia as a witch. Clym's announced rational desire is "an attempt to disturb a sequence to which humanity has been long accustomed"—namely, ignorance of itself. Again, he functions as the self-conscious expression of the dramatic impulses brought to life in Eustacia. As if to emphasize Clym's function as her conceptual counterpart, Christian appears with the news that "Susan Nunsuch had pricked Miss Vye with a long stockingneedle" in church directly after Yeobright's attempt to explain to his mother that he wants to teach men "how to breast the misery they are born to."

Clym's return markedly affects Eustacia's life: "her colourless inner world would before night become as animated as water under a microscope." Clym's relationship with her resembles the "propagandists" that Hardy describes as succeeding "because the doctrine they bring into form is that which their listeners have for some time felt without being able to shape." We are told, too, that Clym's mind is not well proportioned, just as Eustacia's is not, although for different reasons. Yeobright seeks to help his fellow men even at the risk of sacrificing himself; while Eustacia claims: "I have not much love for my fellow-creatures. Sometimes I quite hate them."

Hardy's artistic sympathy lies secretly with Eustacia and the early vision of the heath. "In each of these instances Hardy's sympathy, which was the great source of his creative energy, proved more powerful than his clearly defined intentions; his characters did not escape him, but they did escape his didactic view of their problems" (Albert Guerard, *Thomas Hardy*). The "electric light" of Clym's intellect becomes but another community fire that literally blinds him to the darkness—he impairs his eyesight by reading—thought, the "disease of flesh." Just as the community is susceptible to collapse once its fiery illusions have been extinguished, so Clym's passion for Eustacia breaks down Egdon's resistance to the germ within its own nature. Clym's rupture with his mother because of his marriage symbolizes the drift of the action; it is noteworthy, too, that Mrs. Yeobright has been concerned with social forms and conventions throughout the novel. Yeobright's idealized intellectualism is worthless (Hardy as thinker) when confronted with the living force behind his ideas in Eustacia (Hardy as artist).

> If it were not that man is much stronger in feeling than in thought, the Wessex novels would be sheer rubbish, as they are already in parts. . . .

> But it is not as a metaphysician that one must consider Hardy. He makes a poor show there. For nothing is so pitiable as his clumsy efforts to push events into line with his theory of being. . . .
>
> His feeling, his instinct, his sensuous understanding is, however, apart from his metaphysic, very great and deep, deeper than that, perhaps, of any other English novelist. Putting aside his metaphysic, which must always obtrude when he thinks of people, and turning to the earth, to landscape, then he is true to himself.
>
> (D. H. Lawrence, "Study of Thomas Hardy," in *Selected Literary Criticism*)

The logic of plot is identical to the implications of the logic of character. Eustacia acts against Clym's wishes at the crucial moment of his mother's visit to Anglebury. Eustacia consequently assumes responsibility while Clym suffers; finally, when she receives punishment, he must endure the pain. The full flush of their love occurs during summer on the heath, that deceptive time when Egdon appears gorgeous, but winter is sure to return to reveal once again the bare outlines of man and nature. Almost exactly at the middle of the novel, Hardy describes the landscape against which Clym and Eustacia's love grows "to oppressiveness."

> Everything before them was on a perfect level.
>
> Clym watched her as she retired towards the sun . . . As he watched, the dead flat of the scenery overpowered him, though he was fully alive to the beauty of that untarnished early summer green which was worn for the nonce by the poorest blade. There was something in its oppressive horizontality which too much reminded him of the arena of life; it gave him a sense of bare equality with, and no superiority to, a single living thing under the sun.

The seasons, the landscape, and man have moved from the winter of the opening of the novel to this "arena of life": but an overpowering heat pervades this deceptive openness and, like the passion of the lovers, takes Mrs. Yeobright's life.

Bound to the heath, bound to each other, Clym and Eustacia work out the contradictions of a fatal dialectic: her forswearing of compromise, "congenial to philosophy, . . . is apt to be dangerous to the commonwealth"; she feels and acts and is the catalyst for the turn of the action.

Clym thinks, but remains blind to the true mysteries of the heath, like his mother and the rustics. Artist triumphs over thinker as flesh triumphs over spirit. The battle of "the mutually destructive interdependence of spirit and flesh" in the mind of the author can only bind itself to the invocation of the opening pages of the novel: "the hitherto unrecognized original" becomes "the return of the repressed" and informs the imaginative universe in deed. Clym, while intellectually harassed by "the irrepressible New," still cannot feel the recognition of its power because he was born to the heath and, as a result, must remain blind to it. Eustacia, the intruder, surveys Egdon from the hilltop and unthinkingly responds to its darkest impulses in her feelings and actions.

Clym's view of the heath, especially as an "arena of life" and as an open vista of apparently clear consciousness, is a function of his own perceptions; just as Eustacia's kinship to the wild and craglike winter heath of the first book draws the firmest lines of her character. Thomasin and Venn's ability to make their way about the heath as natives, without fear and with only their conscious intentions directing them, reflect at a distance Clym's original nature. Had Yeobright never gone to Paris, he would not have been attractive to Eustacia—nor, in metaphorical translation, would he ever have become her conceptual counterpart. Thus, Hardy's imagination is impelled to creation by necessary tensions: the electric light of reason, and thought, a disease of the flesh (Clym), are ranged against the hitherto unrecognized original of the central valley, the secret recesses of sensuousness (Eustacia).

The importance of *The Return of the Native* lies in its discovery that the source of the community's potential for downfall lies within the deep recesses of the nature of society itself. The device of the outside intruder has become a catalyst rather than a cause. The marriage between Venn and Thomasin at the end of the novel is as false as Clym's becoming a preacher; as Hardy joins the devil's party, each new insight triggers such repressive responses. With his next book, however, a sustained vision will finally emerge from the combat of the past.

Landscape with Figures

Ian Gregor

There are not many things which can be said with safety about *The Return of the Native,* but one which can is that the novel which Hardy began in the early part of 1877 was very different from the novel which we now know under that title. With the public success of *Far from the Madding Crowd* in mind Hardy decided, after the dubious experiment in social satire represented by *The Hand of Ethelberta,* to return to Wessex and write a novel similar in substance if not in mood to *Far from the Madding Crowd.* With some fifteen chapters completed he followed his previous practice and sent the new novel off to Leslie Stephen for publication in the *Cornhill.*

Stephen, however, had his misgivings, feeling "the story might develop into something dangerous for a family magazine," and he refused to commit himself to publication until he could see the completed novel. It would seem that at this point Hardy subjected his manuscript to basic revision, though he felt no inclination to resubmit the result to Stephen. Beginning his revision in the shadow of Bowdler, Hardy became so caught up in the process that, not only did the whole story emerge radically revised, but the revision enabled Hardy to discover, for the first time, the extent and depth of his imagined world.

In the original manuscript version of the first fifteen chapters the material was very close to *Far from the Madding Crowd*—Thomasin replaced Fanny Robin, Venn replaced Oak, Wildeve replaced Troy, and a more darkly passionate Eustacia replaced Bathsheba. Eustacia was made to have

---

From *The Great Web: The Form of Hardy's Major Fiction.* Faber & Faber, 1974.

affinities with the demonic version of "la belle dame sans merci" in contrast to the innocent heroine, represented by Thomasin. Clym, at this stage of the composition, had just arrived on the scene and so far as his background is sketched out it is cast in provincial rather than cosmopolitan mood, his success being achieved as a shopkeeper in Budmouth, rather than as a would-be diamond merchant in Paris. At this point Hardy began to revise his manuscript.

It is not difficult to guess the catalyst which began to transform the material. In the fifteenth chapter of the novel Clym's arrival is announced, and it was surely the possibilities which Hardy began to envisage here that made him shift his interest in the earlier material. With all the major characters, except Clym and his mother, Hardy was drawing on versions already created in *Far from the Madding Crowd*. It was simply a question of getting a new "mix." But Clym gave Hardy an opportunity to bring into Wessex not the sophisticated life of *The Hand of Ethelberta* but, much more important for his purposes, a sophisticated consciousness; and with that, his theme—the return of the native—began to shape itself as his central concern. By giving Clym a more travelled, more cosmopolitan background, Hardy can provide himself with the kind of consciousness which, if not authorial, can admit into Wessex a world beyond its boundaries, and, in so doing, can inoculate it against the quaint. Clym comes therefore to take up the central interest; and it is not difficult to see that the demonic element in Eustacia, provoked by her contrast in Thomasin, would have very much more interesting implications if set in contrast to Clym. She would give an added resonance to the notion of "native."

Once a central relationship became established between Clym and Eustacia, the whole novel was likely to be restructured in feeling. The "demonic" side of Eustacia could still exist, but was available for much less literal treatment, and could release more understanding of her nature than could her practices. It was left to people like Susan Nunsuch to respond to the latter and use the needle and make the wax doll. The "representativeness" of Clym begins to have, inevitably, an enlarging significance for the role of Eustacia.

With Clym and Eustacia established as centres of dramatic interest, the other characters begin to be regrouped. Thomasin remains the traduced heroine, but reveals a resilience and toughness not usually associated with that role. Wildeve too is a little altered from the middle-aged philanderer to a younger, sentimental and wayward lover—a much more credible and more sympathetic figure for Eustacia's lover. In some ways it is the successive transformations of Venn—reddleman, "mephistophelean visitant," dairy farmer—that indicate most sharply the variety of imaginative pressures at work in the evolution of the novel. Paterson summarises his account of this evolution by remarking: "The process exemplifies . . . the gradual and painful emergence of consciousness out of unconsciousness: the novel turns out to have been quite as much the product of revision as the product of vision. Up to a certain point, the work of a powerful imagination not fully aware of its own nature, it comes increasingly to be the work of an imagination awake to, and in control of, the possibilities it itself has created. In the chapter that follows I would like to argue that Paterson is describing not just "the process of revision" but the novel's very subject matter. In the actual form of *The Return of the Native* we find, in Arnold's phrase, "the dialogue of the mind with itself."

II

When the reader comes to reflect upon his experience of reading *The Return of the Native* he is left, I think, with the distinct impression that the dramatic life of the novel is most vividly present in the first book, which is dominated by Egdon Heath, and in the fourth book, which brings to a crisis the relationship between Clym and his mother. I think that the relationship between these two books tells us a good deal about the success, and the limitations, of the novel as a whole, and to look at each in turn is to obtain an insight into the peculiar nature of this novel.

It is a routine gesture by now to refer to that "vast tract of unenclosed wild known as Egdon Heath" as "the chief character in the novel." If the claim is made as a way of registering the significance of the Heath as a presence throughout the novel, then it is difficult to dispute its justice. But it is a formulation which raises in a direct way the difficulty inherent in any discussion of the Heath—the difficulty present in that transition from "land" to "character." We have continuously to keep in mind that whatever metaphysical airs blow across the Heath, whatever interest there may be in Hardy's speculation that it may be the Heath of that traditionary King of Wessex—Lear, Egdon is very much a tract of land, upon which people constantly walk, and have their houses, little more than pinpoints of light in an enveloping darkness. "Blooms-End," "Mistover-Knap," "The Quiet Woman," these are the elegaic and sardonic addresses where much of the drama, however epic in scope and intention, is to be located; they are isolated habitations, precariously managing to distinguish themselves from the surrounding Heath. But, in fact, they do succeed, and however much we are aware of the attenuated sense of community in this novel—we seem in a different world from the Wessex of Weatherbury, Casterbridge, Little Hintock—we feel the individual standing out starkly and stubbornly against the soft obliterations of the Heath. It is this tension between "land" and "character" which Hardy takes up at the outset of the novel, and he takes it up not in a metaphysical or psychological way—though those implications are present—but rather as something physically seen and felt. It is through the primal contrast of light and darkness that the novel begins to take shape.

The contrast is present throughout the opening chapters, but its significance can be seen if we look at a sequence of paragraphs in chapter 3, "The Custom of the Country." The first one begins:

> Moreover to light a fire is the instinctive and resistant act of man when, at the winter ingress, the curfew is sounded throughout Nature. It indicates a spontaneous, Promethean rebelliousness against the fiat that this recurrent season shall bring foul times, cold darkness, misery and death. Black chaos comes, and the fettered gods of the earth say, Let there be light.

The tone is epic—we are recalled to the primal opposition between "black chaos" and "Promethean rebelliousness"—and in the first assertion the epic tone becomes biblical. It is a paragraph which leaves me in no doubt that Hardy conceived these opening chapters on the grandest scale; the conflict he intimated could recall the Promethean quest itself, when fire was stolen from the gods to be given to men. It is the myth of man becoming conscious of his own nature and, despite odds, endeavouring to obey what he feels to be his destiny. The movement from "lighting a fire" to "Let there be light" is the proclamation of that destiny, and the paragraph pays its tribute to "the instinctive and resistant act of man."

It is however a paragraph which is succeeded by two others which radically alter the tone. The shift in the second paragraph is from the act of man, man as the bearer and stealer of fire, to man as acted upon, an object upon which the flames are reflected:

> All was unstable; quivering as leaves, evanescent as lightning. Shadowy eye-sockets, deep as those of a death's head, suddenly turned into pits of lustre: a lantern-jaw was cavernous, then it was shining; wrinkles were emphasised to ravines, or obliterated entirely by a changed ray.

This is man as appearance, a grotesque, existing and then being "obliterated" by the play of light and shadow. "Pits," "caverns," "ravines," the human face becomes one with the inanimate world. But such generalised sight begins to focus itself, and out of the darkness comes the face of an old man who was not "really the mere nose and chin that it appeared to be, but an appreciable quantity of human countenance." This is man no longer as pure will, or pure object, but someone "sunning himself in the heat":

> The beaming sight, and the penetrating warmth, seemed to breed in him a cumulative cheerfulness, which soon amounted to delight. With his stick in his hand he began to jig a private minuet . . . he also began to sing.

The fire is now both inside *and* outside the man, it has warmed him into consciousness of himself and he seeks expression in dance and song. But for Hardy, that song can only be personal, and he is not just "man," but a particular old man:

> A fair stave, Grandfer Cantle; but I am afeard 'tis too much for the mouldy weasand of such a old man as you. . . . Dostn't wish wast young again, I say? There's a hole in thy poor bellows nowadays seemingly.

"A hole in thy poor bellows" wryly, almost wittily, catches man's relationship with the fire as Hardy sees it, and in so doing goes back to include all the perspectives which the sequence of paragraphs has suggested. Its gentle note of affectionate humour establishes the encompassing tone of compassion for human frailty, and reminds us not just of the character but of the author.

In the unfolding action of the novel, the episode is a marginal one, but in its own way it reveals a stance and expresses the sense of shifting perspective central to the working of Hardy's imagination. When we think of Egdon it is as "a Titanic form . . . unmoved, during so many centuries," "it had a lonely face, suggesting tragic possibilities," it can give "ballast to the mind adrift on change," but it is also where man has written his distinctive signature across its entire length in the shape of "the white surface of the road." And it is life on the road which also belongs to these opening chapters.

It is on the road, as so often in Hardy, that the human drama begins. Thomasin, distressed by Wildeve's carelessness about the details of their marriage certificate, has run away from him and has been picked up by Venn and taken home in his van. On the way they meet Thomasin's aunt, Mrs. Yeobright, who, although relieved at finding Thomasin safe, nevertheless awaits the explanation of her behaviour with extreme annoyance.

Though it is the presence of Egdon which broods over these opening chapters, it is important to remember that this domestic drama also has its impression to make as we begin to read the novel. On the heath great time-honoured rituals take place with the lighting of the bonfires; on the road there is a precise domestic drama involving the validity of a marriage certificate's being made correctly in terms of time and place. The fire and the certificate initiate the plot of the novel, a plot which men partly make themselves, and partly belong to.

In these opening chapters, however, it is the presence of Egdon which dominates, and geographically and dramatically finds its centre on Rainbarrow, "the pole and axis of this heathery world." From the road a figure can be seen on the summit:

> Such a perfect, delicate, and necessary finish did the figure give to the dark pile of hills that it seemed to be the only obvious justification of their outline. . . . The scene was strangely homogeneous, in that the vale, the upland, the barrow, and the figure above it amounted only to unity.

It is another way, again in sharply visual terms, of expressing the shifting perspectives I described earlier in relation to the fire. Up to this point in the novel the emphasis has been on the timelessness and the emptiness of the Heath, of the way in which it ignores or transcends the individual life. But with this first impression of Rainbarrow we see the human form giving "perfect, delicate, and necessary finish" to "the pole and axis of this heathery world." But then, as soon as we think that form is inseparable from the "motionless structure," it moves and disappears "with the glide of a water-drop down a bud." Its place is taken by the locals who have to prepare and light their bonfire.

For "the observer," however,—that ubiquitous presence in Hardy—the imagination "clung by preference to that vanished, solitary figure, as to something more interesting, more important, more likely to have a history worth knowing than these new-comers." It is an introduction, as prophetic as it is dramatic, to the still-unnamed Eustacia. What it establishes from the start is that our sense of Eustacia is to be intimately bound up with our sense of the Heath. Her drama will not be of a kind where an invalid marriage licence will have an important part to play. As Eustacia is standing motionless on the top of Rainbarrow, Thomasin is lying asleep in Venn's van on the road below, and the vignette is emblematic of the difference between them. For the observer, Thomasin asleep reveals "An ingenuous, transparent life . . . as if the flow of her existence could be seen passing within her." From the start Eustacia is associated with opacity, with night; and from the start too, appearance is not what it seems. "The necessary finish to the hill" only exists in the eye of the observer; for Eustacia, the top of the hill has been chosen to catch the last glimmer of daylight, and her gaze strains to the horizon—if it falls upon Egdon, she feels it falls upon her gaol. The ambiguities which surround Eustacia are made explicit in the reader's formal introduction to her in a chapter significantly titled "Queen of Night."

This chapter once used to furnish extracts for anthologies of English prose, nowadays is more likely to furnish extracts for discussions about Hardy's delusions about "fine writing." Both sets of critics would agree it was highly wrought. For me it is precisely this, the manner of the writing, which constitutes its matter. In another writer, like Flaubert in his description of Emma Bovary, this use of style is readily seen, and it is readily seen because we have come to associate this stylistic irony with impersonal narration. When it occurs in a novel in which the author is vividly present and where the manner of narration is always varying in tone, we are taken by surprise and fail to see the way in which the author has altered his distance from his character. The note of irony struck in the opening sentences is hardly aiming at subtlety of effect:

> Eustacia Vye was the raw material of a divinity. On Olympus she would have done well with a little preparation. She had the passions and instincts which make a model goddess, that is, those which make not quite a model woman. Had it been possible for the earth and mankind to be entirely in her grasp for a while, had she handled the distaff, the spindle, and the shears at her own free will, few in the world would have noticed the change of government.

With that passage in mind we can see why the presentation of Eustacia is more justly thought of as "mock-heroic," than heroic, and a persuasive argument can be advanced along those lines. But that description is rather too sharp, it fails to take into account the shift in tone which takes place in the very next paragraph: "To see her hair was to fancy that a whole winter did not contain darkness enough to form its shadow: it closed over her forehead like nightfall extinguishing the western glow." Here, in a rhythm reminiscent of *Antony and Cleopatra,* Hardy is striking an unequivocally romantic tone. The effect of these different tones is not to create any sense of moral complexity about Eustacia—Hardy is not interested in her in that way—but more simply to assert that there is something about her and the life she leads that makes us think of her as a tragic and beautiful woman, and yet at the same time as a woman whose mind and aspirations are those of a romantic schoolgirl. "There was no middle distance in her perspective, that remark comes close to the centre of Hardy's interest in her, as she wanders the Heath, telescope in one hand, hourglass in the other. Sometimes a single sentence gives us the double tone:

> To be loved to madness—such was her great desire. Love was to her the one cordial which could drive away the eating loneliness of her days. And she seemed to long for the abstraction called passionate love more than for any particular lover.

From one point of view this reads as a judicial description of adolescent fervour, a diagnosis of the source of Eustacia's weakness and one that can only move the author to reproof if not to irony. But from another point of view, it is the "eating loneliness" of Eustacia's days which commands attention, and the absence of "love," whose language alone can help her to an understanding of herself. In one way it is right to think that her "love" is not bound up with a particular person, it is invoked to overcome some deep-seated "malaise" within her about her own identity. "Her appearance accorded well with [her] rebelliousness, and the shady splendour of her beauty was the real surface of the sad and stifled warmth within her." In that remark, untouched by irony, we feel what it is in Eustacia which prompts Hardy's sympathy—a consciousness of the way in which her intensities of feeling, her capacity for response, are never to find satisfactory expression. That such a consciousness can accompany behaviour which is self-deceiving and foolish is not something which Hardy is concerned to deny or to excuse; but equally it is not something which can conceal or dispel the genuine tragedy which is involved.

Hardy's double-visioned view of Eustacia is not there to make her a more complex psychological figure. It is there to render an individual in imaginative terms so that we can see her, simultaneously, as Captain Vye's granddaughter, recklessly summoning her old lover to meet her on the Heath, and also as that anonymous form standing on the top of Rainbarrow, having her days "eaten away" in loneliness. It is a duality of view which is to persist to her death itself, so that we do not know, when she drowns in the weir, whether she accidentally mistook her path on her way to elope with Wildeve, or whether, overcome by weariness and despair, she gave up her life for lost. At one point she exclaims passionately to Wildeve: "But do I desire unreasonably much in wanting what is called life—music, poetry, passion, war, and all the beating and pulsing that is going on in the great arteries of the world?" A question to which there can be no simple answer for Eustacia. Her desire is eminently reasonable in that it reveals her appetite for life; eminently mistaken, in that such an appetite can never be satisfied in terms of the images of romance provided in *The Lady's History* she read at school. The importance of this question to Wildeve goes, however, behind the details of its formulation; it is the existence of such a question which takes us back to the Promethean concern of the opening chapters, and it is in that unformulated drive that Eustacia claims epic status, not in "the dark splendour" of her beauty, and certainly not in the details of her behaviour.

To say all this is not to say that Hardy was entirely successful in his aim, but it suggests ways in which Hardy thought of "character." In the last analysis, it seems to me that to use a term like "mock-heroic" as descriptive of the presentation of Eustacia as the "Queen of Night," while it might enable laudatory or disparaging estimates of Eustacia to be bypassed, nevertheless suggests a reconciliation of the conflicting impulses in terms which belong too exclusively to a moral plane. Hardy's interest in Eustacia is more existential than that, and can be brought out only when she is seen in conjunction with Clym. It is his consciousness which predicates hers, as almost certainly Hardy saw it would do, when he began his revision of the first fifteen chapters. Before we go on to a consideration of this relationship, however, something remains to be said about Hardy's "fine writing" in this episode.

For those critics who find Hardy's writing less than fine in this chapter, there has been one sentence in particular which they have felt eloquently illustrative. Describing Eustacia's face Hardy says: "Viewed sideways, the closing-line of her lips formed, with almost geometric precision, the curve so well known in the arts of design as the cima-recta, or ogee." Admittedly, it is not a sentence remarkable for its felicity, but before wishing it away, it is worth pausing and asking what Hardy is trying to do here. It is perhaps the most extreme example in the chapter of those ostentatious references to the fine arts which characterise so many of Hardy's pages. It is usually considered that this is Hardy simply trying to win golden opinions, either for Eustacia, or for himself as "a man of culture"—and not merely as someone "who was a good hand at a serial," but as "a man of culture." With regard to the first, we have seen that Hardy is not really concerned with Eustacia in the way that would give meaning to "opinions," golden or otherwise. With regard to the second, Hardy's personal relationship with his fiction is so oblique, that to use it for cultural self-advertisement would only have provoked his irony. Hardy's references to artists—and the same applies to all his "cultural" allusions—have a dramatic function rather than a descriptive one. They are employed as means of altering the reader's response, so that he is kept moving, in the way that the novel itself is constantly moving, from a dramatic to a contemplative mood, and then back again. The allusions are one of the means through which Hardy keeps us alert to the mediating consciousness of the author, which is always integral to his meaning. In "Queen of Night," however, the allusions have a more precise function to perform. The novel has begun with Egdon, finding in Eustacia its apparent queen, "standing silently on its highest point." As the novel has unfolded we find that, far from being "queen of the solitude," Eustacia is in fact its prisoner. In this chapter Hardy dramatises the paradox. The Queen of Night is, in imagination, a Queen of the Salon, her desired setting is not the Heath, but Bourbon roses, rubies, the march in "Athalie"; and if there has to be a moon behind her head, then it had better be the kind that passes muster on "many respected canvases."

The effect is analagous to that which I have been looking at throughout the chapter. At one level the baroque frame which Hardy put round his picture is a wry comment on the particular aspirations of *his* Queen of Night, but at the same time it is expressive on a consciousness trying to wrest a meaning out of a world where "the clothing of the earth is primitive" and where "swarthy monotony" predominates. For Hardy's "Queen of Night," the Promethean quest is not to be found in fire, but in works of artifice. She herself would like to be thought of as one—"viewed sideways, the closing-line of lips formed, with almost geometric precision. . . ." Hardy does not, of course, succeed here, the strengths of his imagination lay in other directions; but he was attempting something integral to his whole plot, and to see the change of style in this chapter as incidental, an indulgence in "fine writing," is to miss the point as completely as if we were to identify Eustacia's viewpoint with that of her creator, and confuse her "high gods" with his.

At the beginning of this chapter, I suggested there were two areas of the novel which lingered in the mind as possessing distinctive dramatic life. The first is Egdon Heath and Eustacia's relationship with it. The second, is the relationship between Clym and his mother, particularly as it approaches its crisis, where Eustacia has her own vital role to play. Where the first episode moves, as we have seen by resonance and fluent transition, the second is a fine instance not so much of sequence as of consequence. It is in the precise trajectory of plot that we find the significance of the episode as it gathers around impressions, not of a timeless region and hopeless aspiration, but in the history of the individual heart.

There is a particular point in this second episode where the difference in feeling from the opening chapters becomes immediately apparent. Clym and Eustacia have just got married, and the July sun is shining over their small cottage on Egdon: "The heath and changes of weather were quite blotted out from their eyes for the present. They were enclosed in a sort of luminous mist, which hid from them surroundings of any inharmonious colour, and gave to all things the character of light." The "luminous mist" is a natural consequence of their newfound happiness, but it indicates a self-absorption which we are quickly told has the danger of "consuming their mutual affection at a fearfully prodigal rate." It is this absorption, mutual though it is, which leads them on increasingly to emphasise their own wishes, careless of the fact that these are not also the wishes, or at least the consents, of the other. Clym becomes ever more intransigent about devoting himself to life on the Heath; Eustacia, no less intransigent about escaping from it. From desire to assertion; we find Clym singing to himself in defiant contentment as he works on as a furze-cutter; we find Eustacia bored to distraction, seeking relief at a nearby dance and finding Wildeve there:

> The enchantment of the dance surprised her. A clear line of difference divided like a tangible fence her experience within this maze of motion from her experience without it. Her beginning to dance had been like a change of atmosphere; outside, she had been steeped in arctic frigidity by comparison with the tropical sensations here. She had entered the dance from the troubled hours of her late life as one might enter a brilliant chamber after a night walk in a wood.

That inner dislocation of experience is to be fatal for Eustacia, as she retreats ever further from what she feels to be "the arctic frigidity" of her marriage into "the brilliant chamber" of her own reveries. Widening the dislocation between Clym and Eustacia and giving it a language in which to express itself, there is Mrs. Yeobright's attitude to the marriage of her son.

For several months, Mrs. Yeobright had been bitterly opposed to Eustacia, offering first one reason and then another to Clym as justification for her attitudes. We are made to feel, however, that the reasons simply act as a cover for an innate antagonism towards anyone who competes for Clym's love. Clym feels profoundly for his mother and, in a passage strangely prophetic of moments in *Sons and Lovers,* Hardy describes their relationship:

> The love between the young man and his mother was strangely invisible now. Of love it may be said, the less earthly the less demonstrative. In its absolutely indestructible form it reaches a profundity in which all exhibition of itself is painful. It was so with these. Had conversations between them been overheard, people would have said, "How cold they are to each other!"
>
> His theory and his wishes about devoting his future to teaching had made an impression on Mrs. Yeobright. Indeed, how could it be otherwise when he was a part of her—when their discourses were as if carried on between the right and the left hands of the same body? . . . From every provident point of view his mother was so undoubtedly right, *that he was not without a sickness of heart in finding he could shake her.*[My italics.]

It is not difficult to see, with a passage like this in mind, that Clym, in going against his mother and marrying Eustacia, is almost willing his own self-destruction, driving a splinter between "the right and the left hands of the same body." It is a passage which casts light on Clym's relationship with Eustacia, a relationship significantly only rarely described from his point of view until it reaches its full development; and then, as so often in Hardy, it is already beginning to decline, finding expression only in the accents of bitterness and regret. The nature of the rent that parting from his mother makes in Clym's nature finds immediate expression on the night he leaves her. It is described, obliquely in terms of an enclosure of fir and beech trees, which Clym passes on his way to his new cottage, an enclosure planted in the year of Clym's birth:

> The wet young beeches were undergoing amputations, bruises, cripplings, and harsh lacerations, from which the wasting sap would bleed for many a day to come, and which would leave scars visible till the day of their burning. Each stem was wrenched at the root, where it moved like a bone in its socket, and at every onset of the gale convulsive sounds came from the branches, as if pain were felt.

Clym's grief is for him the grief of the world; but we see that, in his case, the enlargement is working in the opposite direction from the way in which Egdon enlarged—and defined—the aspirations and needs of Eustacia. The mood there was to take the fire out into the darkness, to summon Wildeve out of the night, and to move away from the toils of the enclosed self to an undiscovered country beyond. But for Clym, the convulsive sob of the trees is the weeping within his own heart. In marrying Eustacia, Clym severs himself not only from his mother, but from his own being: "He kissed her cheek, and departed in great misery. . . . The position had been such that nothing more could be said without, in the first place, breaking down a barrier; and that was not to be done." The division between them has passed beyond articulation, speech can no longer carry, and when Mrs. Yeobright comes to knock unavailingly at the closed door of Clym's house, she is at a barrier long since constructed between them. The knock sounds only in the turmoil of his dream.

If we are tempted into thinking of that knock as "a knock of fate," it is worth looking back and seeing how many of the incidents that have led to Mrs. Yeobright's starting out on that fatal walk to Clym's cottage have been characterised by the folly of the participants. Mrs. Yeobright's sustained hostility to Eustacia, though expressed in terms of reason, is founded on baseless suspicion. Her charge that she is indebted to Wildeve for money since her marriage to Clym is the kind of insult impossible to overlook. When she thinks of sending the money to Thomasin she entrusts it to the unreliable Christian Cantle, and is indifferent as to whether Thomasin's husband knows about the arrangement or not. Clym's behaviour to Eustacia since his marriage becomes increasingly self-absorbed and boorish, and however much she knew of his desire to remain on Egdon, she can never have anticipated his total obsession with it, matched by total indifference to her own wishes. He can only begin to communicate with her in terms of moral rebuke: "Has your love for me all died, then, because my appearance is no longer that of a fine gentleman." Eustacia herself, though more sinned against than sinning in these later stages, nevertheless makes no attempt to do anything except reiterate her constant desire to escape from Egdon; but given the circumstances of an implacably hostile mother-in-law, and a husband who spends sixteen hours a day cutting furze, and sleeps largely for the remainder, it is not difficult to sympathise with her wish. It may be argued by way of defence that the reason for Clym's absorption in his work on the Heath is his failing eyesight, but although this is certainly presented as a fact, the impression it makes, dramatically, is oddly perfunctory. It comes to seem more of an expression of Clym's inner failings than a fact in its own right, existing much in the way Mrs. Yeobright intends when she remarks about Eustacia, "You are blinded, Clym. . . . It was a bad day for you when you first set eyes on her."

Given that it is possible to offer such an account of personal folly, we must go on to ask why it is that when we come to the climactic episode—the walk across the Heath, the closed door, the fatal return—we forget this to such a degree that we begin to think in terms of Tragic Fate and a Malevolent Universe. Hardy manages an extraordinarily skilful change of mood, so that it is not too much to say that when Mrs. Yeobright starts out on that walk she is, in our imagination, an elderly, embittered woman, often the victim of her own folly. When, later in the day, the heathdwellers gather round her, as she lies exhausted and dying, we feel in the presence of a tragedy, which is much more than an individual one.

It might be said that the transforming factor lies simply in the suffering that the episode involves, but while this is certainly true, it can only be a partial truth. If we assent to that suffering, and feel moved by it, it is only because it is psychologically and dramatically coherent with what has gone before. Hardy has been able to reveal in this episode a new dimension in the previous catalogue of individual folly, and give it the status of genuine tragedy.

The central moment in the scene occurs below the level of wakeful consciousness—when Clym, dimly roused by the knock on the door, stirs in his sleep and murmurs, "mother." Eustacia hears his murmur, concludes he is awake and will answer the knock on the door. It is from her misinterpretation and her failure to check on her impression that the tragedy arises.

The episode exposes with startling clarity that element in Hardy which Virginia Woolf described as "the margin of the unexpressed." Below the pettiness, the egotism and the sheer folly of the quarrels between the Yeobrights, there are great surges of feeling which escape this kind of naming. It is these feelings which the scene on the Heath brings into view, and reveals, not in the language of metaphor and allusion, but in the detail of the unfolding narrative. Indeed it is the very "factuality" of the scene which contributes to its almost hallucinatory intensity. The mood is set in the opening sentence:

> Thursday, the thirty-first of August, was one of a series of days during which snug houses were stifling, and when cool draughts were treats; when cracks appeared in clayey gardens, and were called "earthquakes" by apprehensive children; when loose spokes were discovered in the wheels of carts and carriages and when stinging insects haunted the air, the earth and every drop of water that was to be found.

Aridity within and without—the parched throat and the cracks in the earth—this is the mood of foreboding in which the episode is to take place. In this light the eye observes, with extraordinary intentness, the surfaces of things, so that "seeing" becomes a way of "seeing through." When Mrs. Yeobright observes Clym on the Heath, "not more distinguishable from the scene around him than the green caterpillar from the leaf it feeds on," she sees not so much a figure at work on the Heath as the Heath at work upon him: "He appeared as mere parasite of the heath, fretting its surface in his daily labour as a moth frets a garment, entirely engrossed with its products, having no knowledge of anything in the world but fern, furze, heath, lichens, and moss." This is not the intensity of awareness, but drugged absorption, seeking to forget the wound his mother's absence has caused. Even his sleep is torpid, and as with the fir trees Hardy expresses the inner landscape in terms of the outer one:

> There lay the cat asleep on the bare gravel of the path, as if beds, rugs, and carpets were unendurable. . . . A small apple tree, of the sort called Ratheripe, grew just inside the gate, the only one which throve in the garden, by reason of the lightness of the soil; and among the fallen apples on the ground beneath were wasps rolling drunk with the juice, or creeping about the little caves in each fruit which they had eaten out before stupefied by its sweetness.

The cat's sleep, Clym's sleep, a common feeling encloses them—a feeling here expressed in terms of fecundity and decay, "the smooth surface" and "the little caves . . . eaten out." And so it is with the cottage itself which slumbers in the sunlight, but nurses a turmoil of destructive feeling within. When Mrs. Yeobright's knock comes it dramatically "freezes" the scene, and for an instant the emotional complex of the Yeobrights and Wildeve is laid bare. There is Clym self-absorbed, but inwardly disturbed by his mother's knock; Mrs. Yeobright vainly trying to claim his conscious attention; Eustacia torn between her attentions to Clym and her attentions to Wildeve, fatally indecisive, a pale face at a window, at once custodian and prisoner; Wildeve, impetuous in his arrival, prudent and submissive in his willingness to depart. In a shuttered house on the Heath, far removed in mood from the cosmic sweep of Rainbarrow, the private history of the novel reaches its crisis. Outside, the scene is indistinguishable from what it was before Mrs. Yeobright knocked, "by the scraper, lay Clym's hook and the handful of faggot-bonds he had brought home; in front . . . the empty path, the garden gate standing slightly ajar; and, beyond, the great valley of purple heath thrilling silently in the sun." The only distinction from the earlier scene is that the observing eyes are those now of Eustacia. It is the only distinction that matters.

"Mrs. Yeobright was gone"—rejected by a "pale face at a window" and by the silence of her son. That indeed would be Mrs. Yeobright's account of the incident, but throughout this whole episode Hardy is giving access to a consciousness in the Yeobrights which they themselves only dimly apprehend, if at all. The people involved in the situation begin to feel an odd self-estrangement, expressed lightly in Johnny Nunsuch's remark to Mrs. Yeobright as she walks back from the cottage, that he once, looking at a pond, "seed myself looking up at myself and I was frightened." And it is in that state of suspended consciousness that Mrs. Yeobright, lying back on the bank, sees a colony of ants "never-ending and heavy-laden." Their movement reminds us of the way she once saw communities "from a distance . . . vast masses of beings, jostling, zigzagging, and processioning in definite directions, but whose features are indistinguishable" in the "very comprehensiveness of the view." They remain to her anonymous, oppressive, she can live only at the nerve's end of the individual history, and that nerve would seem to have been severed. She longs to escape the world.

> While she looked a heron arose . . . and flew on with his face to the sun. He had come dripping wet from some pool in the valleys, and as he flew the edges and lining of his wings, his thighs, and his breast were so caught by the bright sunbeams that he appeared as if formed of burnished silver. Up in the zenith where he was seemed a free and happy place, away from all contact with the earthly ball to which she was pinioned; and she wished that she could arise uncrushed from its surface and fly as he flew then.

In this response to the pain her son's seeming desertion has given her, she reacts in the opposite way to Clym. Where he finds in Heath "a soothing self-absorption," she can only feel herself "pinioned," where he loses himself in torpor, she seeks the self-extinction of activity. In both cases, however, they have lost that tension between "character" and "land" which the novel poses as a necessary condition for human equilibrium. These concluding images open perspectives very different from those seemingly announced in that opening sentence, "Thursday, the thirty-first of August, was one of those days . . . "; but the overall movement of this episode has made it possible, and by filling in "the margin of the unexpressed," Hardy has added an insight into human folly, and stature to people who are otherwise perversely self-willed, without in any way mitigating those failures.

We have an opportunity to judge how far Hardy has been successful in this when, soon after Mrs. Yeobright's departure, Eustacia comes to reflect on her role in these proceedings.

> She had certainly believed that Clym was awake, and the excuse would be an honest one as far as it went; but nothing could save her from censure in refusing to answer at the first knock. Yet, instead of blaming herself for the issue she laid the fault upon the shoulders of some indistinct, colossal Prince of the World, who had framed her situation and ruled her lot.

The interesting thing about this authorial intervention is our reaction to it. Earlier in this episode, we would have been moved simply to agree, but now we can feel that, while Eustacia's rhetoric has its own romanticism, the crisp authorial alternative, "instead of blaming herself," will not do either. The effect of the journey on the Heath has not been to alter our view about the folly of the characters and their self-engrossment, but to have softened outlines, to have established "a blur of indistinctness," so that we can see "our will" not operating certainly at the command of a Prince of the World, but not operating either in the lucidities of its own devising. It is a supreme irony that any sentence in Hardy should provoke us into arguing for a more guarded view of the autonomy of the individual will; that one should do so, should alert us to the too easy intervention of the authorial voice.

With the death of Mrs. Yeobright the episode closes, and it is significant that though Hardy seeks an emotional intensity in Clym's denunciation of Eustacia, it disintegrates largely into rant. It comes to that because there has never been any intensity of feeling between them in the first place; its absence has been masked by the vehemence of Mrs. Yeobright's opposition, which has helped to create in the reader's mind a feeling between Clym and Eustacia which has never really been there. With his mother dead, all Clym's feelings are directed towards her, for Eustacia he has only condemnation, and a recanting letter which, almost perfunctorily, goes astray. There is however one moment—significantly it is the moment of Eustacia's departure from Clym—where genuine feeling breaks through and finely reveals Hardy's feeling *for* his characters as well as with them:

> She hastily dressed herself, Yeobright moodily walking up and down the room the whole of the time. At last all her things were on. Her little hands quivered so violently as she held them to her chin to fasten her bonnet that she could not tie the strings,

> and after a few moments she relinquished the attempt. Seeing this he moved forward and said, "Let me tie them."

It recalls another moment when Eustacia's hands were very much under her control, and when it was a favour to be allowed even to touch them. Charley has claimed his "payment" for getting her into the mummer's play; he takes her hand in both of his

> with a tenderness beyond description, unless it was like that of a child holding a captured sparrow.
>
> "Why! there's a glove on it!" he said in a deprecating way.
>
> "I have been walking," she observed.
>
> "But, miss!"
>
> "Well—it is hardly fair." She pulled off the glove, and gave him her bare hand.
>
> They stood together minute after minute, without further speech, each looking at the blackening scene, and each thinking his and her own thoughts.
>
> "I think I won't use it all up tonight," said Charley devotedly.

I instance these two moments because they would not usually get into any formal account of the novel, and yet they seem to me to release a feeling, uniquely Hardy's, and one essential to our experience of his power as a novelist. Though the mood of the two is very different, they both have a mute appeal of one person to another, a tenderness quite free from mawkishness. The scenes have a point beyond their immediate setting in that they serve as a reminder of how much Hardy is concerned with the individual response, and it is this which underlies the historical sweep of his imagination and gives it poignancy.

If then *The Return of the Native* draws its strength from the cosmic perspective seen from Egdon, we have also to say that it draws its strength from the individual histories of the Yeobrights, reaching their climax in a shuttered room. But the overall structure of the novel demands that we go on to ask what relationship exists between these contrary perspectives. We come back to a question I proposed at the outset about the relationship of "land" to "character," or to put it in the more precise terms encouraged by this novel, what kind of a man is the native, and what does he return for?

At the beginning of this chapter I suggested that one of the features that distinguished *The Return of the Native* from *Far from the Madding Crowd* was its concern with forms of consciousness. In the two extended episodes I have looked at, consciousness has been present in terms of place and in terms of individual relationships, but of all Hardy's novels, with the exception of *Jude, The Return of the Native* is the most preoccupied with a social consciousness. Clym we might go on to say is a forerunner of Jude, but as soon as the matter is put like that, we begin to have certain hesitations about the kind of consciousness he embodies and, as a consequence, the consciousness of the novel also.

Clym's decision to remain in Egdon and not return to Paris is announced in a conversation he is having with the locals:

> "I was endeavouring to put off one sort of life for another sort of life, which was not better than the life I had known before. It was simply different."
>
> "True; a sight different," said Fairway.
>
> "Yes, Paris must be a taking place," said Humphrey. "Grand shop-winders, trumpets, and drums; and here be we out of doors in all winds and weathers——"
>
> "But you mistake me," pleaded Clym. "All this was very depressing. But not so depressing as something I next perceived—that my business was the idlest, vainest, most effeminate business that ever a man could be put to. That decided me: I would give it up and try to follow some rational occupation among the people I knew best, and to whom I could be of most use. I have come home . . . I shall keep a school. . . . "
>
> " 'Tis good-hearted of the young man," said another. But, for my part, I think he had better mind his business."

Clym's "business" is not something which is easy to respond to, and this passage indicates the difficulty. It is clear why Clym should find his work in Paris—"making" as Fairway puts it "a world-wide name for yourself in the nick-nack trade"—an idleness and an affront to his notion of what is fitting for a man of education. And it is not difficult to see that coming home to extend the awareness of "the Egdon eremites" in the way the world is going is "fitting" in a way that his work in Paris can never be. Nevertheless, we feel that Fairway has a sharper perception of the gulf that separates Clym from them than he has; in their bluff but general replies to him, there is a firmer grasp of social realities than any exhibited by their teacher, in the sense that they feel his aim, "I shall keep a school," less potent in effecting change than he does. But by the time we come to the end of the passage, we feel that their dismissal of Clym, simply in terms of goodheartedness and their too easy conviction that he should mind his own business, is too patronising, too complacent. The effect on the reader of the passage as a whole is a switchback of sympathies, not because of some complexity within Clym, but because there seems to be some hesitation within the author himself as to just what to make of that decision to "come home." We recall an early moment in the introduction of Clym to the reader:

> In Clym Yeobright's face could be dimly seen the typical countenance of the future. Should there be a classic period to art hereafter, its Pheidias may produce such faces. The view of life as a thing to be put up with, replacing that zest for existence which was so intense in early civilizations, must ultimately enter so thoroughly into the constitution of the advanced races that its facial expression will become accepted as a new artistic departure.

This description directs our attention to the gap between nature and nurture, seen here is the difference between this face and "the face on which time makes no impression"; the contrast is striking, and Hardy is at some pains to make it so. Clym registers in his face the cost of self-awareness, and for Hardy, this is an inescapable part of the evolution of human consciousness, as much a fact as "the vast tract of unenclosed land." And he seems to be saying further that it is the artists who have helped to make us aware of this: each age needs its own Pheidias. But Clym's face is not a passive register recording endurance of "life as a thing to be put up with," it seeks to shape life, to give it meaning and, "As is usual with bright natures, the deity that lies ignominiously chained within an ephemeral human carcase shone out of him like a ray." The Promethean urge may be "chained," but it is defiantly present, and it commands Hardy's admiration. This aspect of Clym Hardy presents fully and sympathetically, and trying to characterise it, we could say that it is his recognition of the needs and the power of the human mind. But within the recognition lies a more uncompromising assertion, an assertion expressed in the quotation which provides a chapter with its title, "my mind to me a kingdom is," and it is this which constitutes, for Hardy, Clym's real limitation. Basically, it is the imperial claims of "mind" that give the defence of his decision to stay in Egdon its sense of unreality and strain; Clym makes a fatal identification of contemporary consciousness with contemporary "mind." And it is this exclusive emphasis on "mind" that makes him conceive of "coming home"—the return of the native—in terms simply of finding "some rational occupation among the people I knew best."

The consequence of this attitude emerges in two ways. The first lies in his notion that what Egdon needs, above all, is knowledge. The authorial comment is sharp:

> We can hardly imagine bucolic placidity quickening to intellectual aims without imagining social aims as the transitional phase. . . . A man who advocates aesthetic effort and deprecates social effort is only likely to be understood by a class to which social effort has become a stale matter.

The force of "social" is not simply in its conjunction with "effort"; it suggests that knowledge, "aesthetic effort," is not something that can ever be aimed at in isolation, but is itself part of the total consciousness of the age. The second way in which Clym's attitude towards "mind" reveals itself is, significantly enough, in his response to Egdon, which had been "inwoven" with his life. He contemplates it and sees the various attempts which have been made to cultivate it but, "when he looked from the heights . . . he could not help in indulging in *a barbarous satisfaction* (my italics) at observing that, in some of the attempts at reclamation from the waste, tillage, after holding on for a year or two, had receded again in despair, the ferns and furze-tufts stubbornly reasserting themselves." Intellectuality is partnered by primitivism, a heady brew for the sophisticated, and stirred up in Clym's case because, between "the kingdom of the mind," and "the vast tract of unenclosed land," there is nothing that can lay claim to his imagination. He is trapped between two versions of experience, "I shall keep a school" and "barbarous satisfaction" at the domination of the Heath over man's attempts at cultivation. For him "character" and "land" remain disjunct, and when he is made to feel the conflict between them, then he becomes radically self-estranged.

The first intimation of this conflict comes when he makes his successful proposal to Eustacia:

> This was the end of their talk, and Eustacia left him. Clym watched her as she retired towards the sun. The luminous rays wrapped her up with her increasing distance, and the rustle of her dress over the sprouting sedge and grass died away. As he watched, the dead flat of the scenery overpowered him, though he was fully alive to the beauty of that untarnished early summer green which was worn for the nonce by the poorest blade. There was something in its oppressive horizontality which too much reminded him of the arena of life; it gave him a sense of bare equality with, and no superiority to, a single living thing under the sun.

It is a strange, almost hallucinatory, passage in which Clym is made to feel a disorientation in his decision to marry Eustacia. He is made to feel in "the bare equality" of the Heath a force which has laid siege to the "kingdom of the mind." It is a force which he feels drains him of individuality, and leaves him vulnerable to his mindless absorption in the land. He can no longer "look down from the heights . . . in barbarous satisfaction," the land in its "oppressive horizontality" overpowers him and he gives his body over to the Heath—and to Eustacia. After the threat to his sight, he retreats into himself, so that he becomes virtually inseparable from the Heath:

> He was a brown spot in the midst of an expanse of olive-green gorse, and nothing more. . . . His daily life was of a curious microscopic sort, his whole world being limited to a circuit of a few feet from his person. His familiars were creeping and winged things, and they seemed to enroll him in their band.

As he becomes one with "the creeping and winged things," the proud isolation of "mind" fades, and there is an accompanying estrangement, first from his mother and then from his wife.

It has been argued that this collapse of Clym's is only a stage in his progress and that, after the tragic deaths of his mother and Eustacia, he recovers. To some extent this is, of course, true. He does emerge from the life of the furze-cutter and he overcomes that consciousness of vast impassivity that the Heath induces in him, so that by the end he can climb Rainbarrow Hill, as Eustacia had done, and once again "look down from the heights." There is a resolution here, but it is difficult to see a vindication. For one thing his behaviour prior to his new career as an itinerant preacher has not been of a kind to win much sympathy: he remains morose, morbidly self-righteous and self-pitying. The fruit of his reading would seem to have left him with the fear that his life may be invaded by a proposal of marriage from Thomasin. When he discovers that Thomasin wishes to marry Venn, who has just saved his life, he can only remark that she might have made a better match. These are hardly the attitudes which an author, anxious to show the ennoblement of his hero through suffering, would put on display. On the other hand, there is no suggestion of hypocrisy or humbug about Clym's adoption of the life of an itinerant preacher, and Clym, as he stands "a motionless figure" on the top of Rainbarrow, is meant to command something of the sympathy, certainly the seriousness, which Eustacia commanded in a similar position at the beginning of the novel.

The cause of the uncertainty in these final stages of Clym's career seems to me that he has become, for Hardy, less and less a character and more and more the embodiment of a dilemma; for his problems are those of his creator. Dramatically, he has been kept alive by his relationship with his mother and Eustacia: they are now dead. Conceptually he has been kept in control because he embodied a contemporary consciousness which, however, really existed only at the level of statement. This is revealed in the concluding authorial comment, where we feel a fatigue about the first sentence in striking contrast to the bracing analysis with which Clym was first introduced:

> Some believed him, and some believed not; some said that his words were commonplace, others complained of his want of theological doctrine; while others again remarked that it was well enough for a man to take to preaching who could not see to do anything else. But everywhere he was kindly received, for the story of his life had become generally known.

But behind this official invitation to make what you like of Clym's life at the end, there is an important point for Hardy. That is, quite simply, that Clym should "go in," he is part of the evolving consciousness of the age, and in his presence at the end, there is the tacit belief that a truth about life cannot be adequately expressed by the deaths on the Heath and in Shadwater Weir. That presence is an integral part of Hardy's belief in the future, and though, for Hardy, Clym individually no longer seems able to provide a dramatic endorsement of that, "his story" nevertheless can.

It may well be argued however that, whatever dubieties attend the affirmation present in Clym's life, surely the real affirmation of the novel is to be found in the marriage of Thomasin and Venn. It was a marriage which provoked Hardy into being his own editor. At the end of the penultimate chapter there appears the following footnote:

> The writer may state here that the original conception of the story did not design a marriage between Thomasin and Venn. He was to have retained his isolated and weird character to the last, and to have disappeared mysteriously from the heath, nobody knowing whither—Thomasin remaining a widow. But certain circumstances of serial publication led to a change of intent.
>
> Readers can therefore choose between the endings, and those with an austere artistic code can assume the more consistent conclusion to be the true one.

It is a remarkable note for an author to make, virtually disavowing his final chapter, and yet nevertheless continuing to retain it in successive editions, long after the "circumstances of serial publication" had been forgotten. It could be argued that once Hardy had given his novel this particular ending it was hard for him to change it, however much he was inclined in that direction; I think however that, if we see the problem in the context of the novel as a whole, it becomes another instance of Hardy's genuine uncertainty about what does constitute the appropriate ending. And we can read the footnote as part of the text, dramatising that uncertainty.

The title of the first chapter of the last book—"The Inevitable Movement Onward"—announces the difficulty. For readers who have what Hardy describes sympathetically as "an austere artistic code" that title can only be a matter for regret, there being no movement "onward" in the disappearance of Venn and in Thomasin's widowhood. But for Hardy such a movement is central to his imaginative undertaking. To have left Thomasin as a widow, when throughout the book she has provided a centre of gravity from which other, more notable characters, have continually departed, would be to give the deaths on the weir and on the Heath a cosmic inevitability which much of the book is concerned to deny. We are continually made to feel that there is a life which extends beyond that of the central characters, and it is Thomasin who helps to give that central drama an important frame. Alone of her family she will not be deceived by false lights on Egdon:

> The drops which lashed her face were not scorpions, but prosy rain; Egdon in the mass was no monster whatsoever, but impersonal open ground. Her fears of the place were rational, her dislikes of its worst moods reasonable.

For someone whose face can reveal "an ingenuous, transparent life . . . as if the flow of her existence could be seen passing within her," Edgon is neither a gaol nor an arcady. To make such a figure finally isolated would be alien to important authorial concerns in the novel, the kind of concerns which, in a much more calculated way, Elizabeth-Jane expresses in *The Mayor of Casterbridge.* Thomasin's final accommodation within the social structure enables Hardy to offer us a perspective on the tragic deaths in the novel which her isolation would deny him, a perspective which reveals an element of folly in their tragedy.

That Venn should be Thomasin's partner in marriage is inevitable if she is to marry at all. She owes her survival largely to his help, and their particular coming together strikes that note which Hardy was so anxious to strike at the end of another relationship of waiting and caring. We could say of Thomasin and Venn, as Hardy said of Bathsheba and Oak, that their romance had grown up "in the interstices of a mass of hard prosaic reality."

It is that note which has to be sounded, because it conveys so distinctly the endurance that for Hardy is the dynamic behind "the inevitable movement onward," an endurance which is not a passive resistance but a shrewd responsiveness to the way things are. Venn "endures" in that he waits with unflagging patience for Thomasin, but it is a patience continuously sustained by energy and enterprise.

Having said these things, however, it is not difficult to see what it is in the marriage between Thomasin and Venn which makes Hardy so uneasy about its serving as a conclusion to the novel. It is too simply emblematic, and even conceding that it is related to Hardy's purpose in the way I have suggested, it is a way which is only marginally connected to the dramatic life of the novel. It belongs much more happily to the simpler fictional world of *Far from the Madding Crowd,* where to acquire, within a few pages, money, fifty cows and a farm would not be too closely inquired into. But Venn's transformation from reddleman to dairy-farmer is not really a question of unsatisfactorily bridging a credibility gap. Venn's role in the novel is directly related to the fact that he is a figure of the past, a reddleman "filling . . . in the rural world the place . . . the dodo occupied in the world of animals." So far as the reader's response to the novel is concerned Venn remains dyed to the end. Significantly, his wooing of Thomasin begins with a maypole dance at a place where "the instincts of merry England lingered on . . . with exceptional vitality." We must take the author's word for it, it is all he has on offer. The trouble is this. If we find difficulty in accepting the marriage between Thomasin and Venn, and, in consequence, difficulty in seeing it as a resolution to the novel, this is not because it offends our sense of credibility, or more grandly, our "austere artistic code," but that the dramatic life which Hardy has been able to give such a marriage is too frail to provide an effective sense of "the inevitable movement onward" in a novel which contains Egdon Heath and the tragedy of the Yeobrights.

III

> There the form stood, motionless as the hill beneath. Above the plain rose the hill, above the hill rose the barrow, and above the barrow rose the figure. Above the figure was nothing that could be mapped elsewhere than on a celestial globe.
>
> Such a perfect, delicate, and necessary finish did the figure give to the dark pile of hills that it seemed to be the only obvious justification of their outline.

> From a distance there simply appeared to be a motionless figure standing on the top of the tumulus. . . . But now it was fine warm weather, with only a summer breeze blowing, and early afternoon instead of dull twilight. . . . Round him upon the slopes of the Barrow a number of heathmen and women were reclining or sitting at their ease. They listened to the words of the man in their midst, who was preaching.

The two scenes, calculatedly recalling one another, pinpoint the conflict that has operated throughout *The Return of the Native* and which, in various ways, I have tried to illustrate. In the first scene the figure, Eustacia, is imaged as an integral part of the universe she inhabits—at one with the body of the Heath, "whose dark soil," Lawrence wrote, "was strong and crude and organic as the body of a beast." In Eustacia's case, of course, it is a partial irony in that her heart, wherever her body may be, is over the hills and far away. Nevertheless, in her sensuous understanding, she is at one with the Heath. For Clym, the characteristic stance on Rainbarrow is not a tensed silhouette giving "necessary finish . . . to the dark pile of hills," but a "convenient signal to those stragglers who wished to draw near." The Heath is now an arena for discourse, a place where his audience "abstractedly pulled heather, stripped ferns, or tossed pebbles down the slope." It is the daylight world. It is difficult not to feel that, in the logic of the novel, the distinction between the two scenes lies in the evolution of consciousness, and that, for Hardy, the second has come to replace the first. If we feel that Hardy fails to present all this convincingly, however, it is because the dramatic tensions of the novel run in other directions than between time past and time present. They lie, as I have attempted to suggest, between the vast impersonality of the heath and the claustrophobic intensity of the individual relationships of the Yeobrights. This leads to that bifocal view of character, so distinctive a feature of the novel; Eustacia as Queen of Night and as romantic daydreamer; Clym as Prometheus and as a slower-moving scholar gypsy; Mrs. Yeobright as having "singular insight into life," and also "a curate's daughter, who had once dreamt of doing better things." If these contrasting perspectives eventually become unsatisfactory, this is not because of a failure on Hardy's part to give psychological credibility to his characters, but because the underlying dialectic between the cosmic and the personal loses tension and becomes simply flaccid.

About the characters we feel that they become either too self-consciously representative or too self-consciously individual. Of the unfolding narrative, we can say that there is no line of communication between the drama of the Heath and the drama of Clym's cottage. What is missing from both these aspects is that fluent assimilation whereby individual lives can be taken up into a history wider than themselves, and the way in which, in its turn, that wider history can be seen to return them to the sharp particulars of living in this time and that place. At one point in the novel Hardy is very much aware of this and in the long description of Clym he makes it explicit. But it is an awareness which exists only at the level of meditation. By the end of the novel Clym's character has been bifurcated—the morose self-centred widower fearing that Thomasin may make unwelcome demands upon him, the unconvincing cut-out of a contemporary sage being "sometimes secular, and sometimes religious, but never dogmatic." The ironies which attend Clym's presence in the last chapters of the book are Hardy's distress signals about a character who has outstayed his welcome. Clym, who at the beginning of the novel had provided Hardy with an opportunity for dramatising a much more sophisticated consciousness than he had ever attempted before, has by the end come uncomfortably close to simply representing his author's dilemma about the gains and losses inherent in evolving consciousness.

Part of the difficulty for the characters in *The Return of the Native* is not their self-awareness, but a passivity, a passivity which acts in defence of deep self-absorption. The characters tend to perceive that they are acting in two plots, one of their own devising, one of vast impersonal forces, but in this novel they see no relationship between the two. It is precisely this perception which gives Henchard, Tess and Jude their tragic stature and comes to constitute, for Hardy, their "character." These are characters who are prepared to live between two worlds, and though they never achieve a resolution, they become genuinely aware of the tension and in that awareness find wisdom. They find it at least partly because they belong to a world which has a precise *social* history, as well as an individual and a cosmic one. Nowhere is this more sharply revealed than in the crucial role assigned to work in these later novels, work which for Hardy is always a form of learning. When we look at *The Return of the Native* we find that work is either perfunctory or emblematic: Clym as furze-gatherer or preacher; Venn as reddleman or dairy-farmer; Wildeve as engineer or innkeeper; even the locals act really as commentators or messengers and have no independent life of their own such as they had in *Far from the Madding Crowd*. The consequence of this for the characters in *The Return of the Native* is that there is no form of learning which is available to them in public and social terms; they live at extremes where a man can become "a mere parasite of the Heath," or where a woman can observe herself as "a disinterested spectator" and think herself "a sport for heaven," or where both can become screened by "a luminous mist" of mutual regard. The effect of this on the reader is that he takes the tragedy of the novel persistently at one remove from his own situation. When Wildeve and Venn gamble on the Heath for instance, there are considerable issues at stake, but we feel that these are rooted only in the exigencies of the story. Memorable as the episode is, it is self-enclosed, taking place in a never-never land. In the novels to come Hardy will make sure that risks of fortune will be illuminated not by the light of glowworms, but by those of the market place. The tragedy of *The Mayor of Casterbridge* may, like the present novel, conclude on Egdon Heath, but it will begin with a stranger unfolding "five crisp pieces of paper" and throwing down on the tablecloth, "Bank of England notes for five pounds."

If, however, *The Mayor of Casterbridge* is to provide Hardy with fresh possibilities for his art, it would be unjust to *The Return of the Native* to conclude on a note which did not emphasise its own positive achievement. It is a novel which has behind it that moment of imaginative growth revealed in the storm-scene in *Far from the Madding Crowd*—and by giving a new dimension of understanding to region, and human feeling, Hardy has effectively explored the relationship of "the infuriated universe" and that "feeling" which the earlier novel had brought him to ponder. When we compare that storm with the use to which Egdon is put, or compare the treatment of obsessive feeling in Boldwood with that of Mrs. Yeobright, we can see the fresh insight that the later novel has afforded. *Far from the Madding Crowd* has its own particular assurance—there seems nothing as comprehensively sustained in the later novel as the sheep washing and celebratory supper—but in introducing Clym, Hardy has introduced a contemporary consciousness into Wessex, and it is this which takes *The Return of the Native* beyond the range of anything in *Far from the Madding Crowd.* It provides him with a theme as well as a method, and enables him to realise that he can find in fiction expression for questions which not only trouble his characters, but trouble himself; if the resolution he aimed at in the novel fails, in the end, to carry conviction, it was because of its very closeness to irresolutions deep within his own thinking. But the drama on Egdon has shown him that these irresolutions cannot be resolved simply by "taking thought"; it has searched out and tested his dramatic imagination, engaged it at full stretch. In other words, we could say that in *The Return of the Native* Hardy reveals himself as a major novelist; he sees for the first time his fictional world—and sees it whole. He will go on to explore it more deeply, but not more extensively.

The Buried Giant of Egdon Heath

Avrom Fleishman

I tell of Giants from times forgotten,
Those who fed me in former days.
Völuspa Saga

Agog and magog and the round of them agrog. To the continuation of that celebration until Hanandhunigan's extermination!
Finnegans Wake

One would search long for a commentator on *The Return of the Native* who has failed to locate the story of Clym Yeobright and Eustacia Vye in the elaborated space of its landscape. Still it may be said that Egdon Heath has not been recognized as a figure in its own right—in both narrative senses of "figure," as person and as trope. One of the closest observers of the novel, John Paterson, has listed some of the heath's associations: "it is a stage grand enough to bear the weight of gods and heroes, more specifically still, it is the prison-house of Prometheus, the fire-bearing benefactor of mankind." Paterson and others have supported such identifications by quoting the novel's repeated attribution of Promethean characteristics to the major characters. Hardy is never one to make his classical allusions evasively; the demonic rebelliousness of Eustacia and the bonded martyrdom of Clym are steadily projected upon the heath in the mode of scenic amplification. Yet the felt connection between the human actors and their inanimate setting exceeds the scope of metonymic associations like the scene-act ratio of Kenneth Burke. The ruling passions of the protagonists in *The Return* and the awesome powers of the heath need to be treated as forces of a like nature—the heath manifesting the same impulses as do the fictional characters.

To return to the setting of Hardy's first major novel is to seize his imagination at an originative position, where his sense of the past and his complex feelings about modern life intersected at a place with which he identified himself. Throughout his career, Hardy was inclined to express his strong response to the history-laden landscape of his shire in images of a special kind—special, that is, when compared with those of other Victorian novelists but commonplace in the tradition of local observers with a bent for narrative explanation. He was born, it will be recalled, in a cottage on the edge of the fourteen miles or so of high ground that has come to be identified with Egdon Heath, and he built his home, Max Gate, near its southwest flank five years after writing *The Return*. In 1878, the year the novel was published, the Folk-Lore Society was founded in London, and at about this date Hardy joined the Dorset Natural History and Antiquarian Field Club. To the latter he also delivered a paper on "Some Romano-British Relics Found at Max Gate, Dorchester"—found, that is, during the digging of foundations for his house. These delvings in the earth encouraged Hardy in a long series of reflections on the presence underfoot of a many-layered past: beginning as early as the passage in *The Return* on Clym's attendance at the opening of a barrow (bk. 3, chap. 3); continuing with the account of unearthed Roman skeletons in *The Mayor of Casterbridge* (chap. 11); and developing a fine blend of fascination and detachment in poems like "The Roman Gravemounds" and "The Clasped Skeletons."

The sense of the past, it has been abundantly demonstrated, touches Hardy's work at innumerable points, but one may be isolated for the present discussion: his adumbration of an animate (or once-animate) being dormant in the earth, whether in the form of a buried skeleton incarnating the ghosts of the past, or of a quasi-human figure underlying or constituting certain topographical features (usually hills), or of a genius loci residing not in an aerial or other evanescent medium but in the soil of the place itself. It will be seen that some such preternatural beliefs are at work amid the rationalist skepticism which Hardy tried to maintain and that, while his own beliefs are not to be equated with those of the peasants in his tales, his absorption in them resembles the intellectual sympathy which modern anthropologists and folklorists have been recommending.

The prime instances of buried figures in the Hardy country are, quite naturally, those associated with a number of massive formations which surpass anything comparable in the southwest—the region of England perhaps most densely populated by ancient remains. Foremost is Maiden Castle, a Celtic hillfort a few miles south of Dorchester, which Hardy described as "an enormous many-limbed organism of an antediluvian time . . . lying lifeless, and covered with a thin green cloth, which hides its substance, while revealing its contour." Comparable in fame and grandeur is the Cerne Abbas giant, with his club and explicit phallus, on a hill seven miles north of Dorchester in a region Hardy favored for his rambles; it is mentioned in *Tess of the D'Urbervilles* and other writings, most saliently when described by the local peasantry in *The Dynasts* as a malevolent ogre, comparable to Napoleon.

Besides those and other gigantic erections in the vicinity, like Stonehenge, additional outcroppings of the land contour Hardy's writings. In a poem titled "The Moth-Signal," specifically set on Egdon Heath and reminiscent of an incident in the *The Return,* the waywardness of modern domestic life is seen from the perspective of a dweller in the earth:

> Then grinned the Ancient Briton
>   From the tumulus treed with pine:
> "So, hearts are thwartly smitten
>   In these days as in mine!"

Hardy takes up the point of view of an inhabitant of the heath in a more personal way in another poem, "A Meeting with Despair" (noted in the manuscript as set on Egdon Heath):

> As evening shaped I found me on a moor
>   Sight shunned to entertain:
> The black lean land, of featureless contour,
>   Was like a tract in pain.
>
> "This scene, like my own life," I said, "is one
>   Where many glooms abide;
> Toned by its fortune to a deadly dun—
>   Lightless on every side."
>
> . . . .
>
> Against the horizon's dim-discernèd wheel
>   A form rose, strange of mould:
> That he was hideous, hopeless, I could feel
>   Rather than could behold.

Although Hardy metaphorically identifies the pattern and tone of his life with the heath's, he resists the insinuations of the apparition-named "Despair" in the title but referred to only as "the Thing" in the poem itself—

so as to argue that the glowing sunset portends better prospects for the future. In a voice we recognize as that of the stupid giant of fairy tales, his interlocutor replies, "Yea-but await awhile! . . . Ho-ho!— / Now look aloft and see!" More striking, perhaps, than either the poem's finale (with the loss of light and portent of defeat) or the similarities between its treatment of Egdon Heath and the novel's is the encounter with an abiding presence there—the black lean land, featureless, in pain, from which a hideous, hopeless form arises.

These poems call to mind others in which one of the most familiar features of Hardy's style, personification, is employed in its mode of gigantism. The best-known instance of this trope is found in "The Darkling Thrush": "The land's sharp features seemed to be / The Century's corpse outleant." In the periodical publication of the poem, its original title emphasized this figure rather than the thrush: "By the Century's Deathbed" enforces the idea not simply of a localized spirit but of the entire earth as a body suffering a secular decline. A more sharply focused version of this image occurs in the poem "By the Earth's Corpse" (from the same volume as "The Darkling Thrush"), in which Time and "the Lord" conduct a dialogue on the themes of guilt and repetition, while placed like mourners near "this globe, now cold / As lunar land and sea," at some future time "when flesh / And herb but fossils be, / And, all extinct, their piteous dust / Revolves obliviously."

The most highly developed vision of the earth as an organic, vaguely human being is, however, that of *The Dynasts*. A stage direction of the "Fore Scene" is justly famous for its panoramic sweep, anticipating (but still surpassing) the movement of the camera eye in epically scaled movies:

> The nether sky opens, and Europe is disclosed as a prone and emaciated figure, the Alps shaping like a backbone, and the branching mountain-chains like ribs, the peninsular plateau of Spain forming a head. . . . The point of view then sinks downwards through space, and draws near to the surface of the perturbed countries, where the peoples, distressed by events which they did not cause, are seen writhing, crawling, heaving, and vibrating in their various cities and nationalities.

With the return to this vision in the "After Scene," Europe is "beheld again as a prone and emaciated figure. . . . The lowlands look like a grey-green garment half-thrown off, and the sea around like a disturbed bed on which the figure lies." In this instance, human forms in the mass join with geographical features to create the image of a total organism: the earth itself (or its European portion) as a giant, going through the stages of awakening, struggle, and exhaustion—a composite being living out the disturbances and sufferings of humankind.

Is it this (or a related) giant who confronts the reader from the title of the opening chapter of *The Return:* "A Face on which Time makes but Little Impression"? The rhetoric of the so-called pathetic fallacy suggests that it is a creature on the scale of the earth: it "wore the appearance of an instalment of night" and, reciprocally, "the face of the heath by its mere complexion added half an hour to evening." Not only are vital reflexes, human apparel, and personal physiognomy suggested, but the sustained comparison of Egdon Heath and mankind is raised from mere analogy to essential identity:

> It was at present a place perfectly accordant with man's nature—neither ghastly, hateful, nor ugly: neither commonplace, unmeaning, nor tame; but, like man, slighted and enduring; and withal singularly colossal and mysterious in its swarthy monotony. As with some persons who have long lived apart, solitude seemed to look out of its countenance. It had a lonely face, suggesting tragical possibilities.
>
> (bk. 1, chap. 1)

It is on the basis of this profound identity that the epithets used for the heath come to resonate like personal designations: "Haggard Egdon," "the untameable, Ishmaelitish thing that Egdon now was," "the people changed, yet Egdon remained." In the most pathetic of these characterizations, the place is defined in relation to other natural forces in a style usually reserved for romantic ficion: "Then Egdon was aroused to reciprocity; for the storm was its lover, and the wind its friend." But the role hardly suits a figure that has emerged as not merely humanized but on a larger-than-individual scale: "singularly colossal and mysterious in its swarthy monotony." Such a colossus can be a hero only of a special sort.

In inventing the name itself, Hardy seems to have had in mind not a place-name but a personal one. Its closest analogue is a forename: *Egbert,* from Old English *ecg* ("sword") and *bryght* ("bright")—the latter term also appearing in the chief surname used in the novel. *Egdon* would be its derivable opposite: the second syllable is equivalent to *dun,* the word used since Anglo-Saxon times to describe the natural shades of landscape, animals, and atmosphere in a dull, brown grey range. (But compare the Celtic name of Maiden Castle: *imai dun* ["strong hill"].) Etymology resolves nothing, but this name goes beyond the expansive suggestiveness of well-wrought place-names in fiction, encouraging instead the identification of a personal presence by a favored technique of characterization.

If these two processes are indeed comparable—if a somewhat amorphous terrain is presented here in the manner in which fictional characters are conventionally introduced—we shall have to revise our expectations of the role of landscape in the novel more radically than we may be prepared to do. Landscape is not satisfied to act in *The Return of the Native* as a background, with human subjects in the foreground (although some positioning of people against a background of natural elements is at work, e.g., in the chapter entitled "The Figure against the Sky"). Instead, Egdon Heath becomes one of the principal agents of the action, a protagonist in the classical sense of the dramatic actor, and probably the most memorable figure to emerge from the events. The title of the novel has been given some new turns in recent criticism, so as to widen its reference beyond the donnée of Clym's return to Wessex. If its individual implications are taken seriously, the title refers somewhat sardonically to Clym's return to the native state in the course of the action; it also suggests more broadly the heath's renewed prominence in the life of the characters and of the modern age generally. *The Return of the Native* would name, then, a story about Egdon Heath.

The operation of these narrative traits makes the term "personification" no longer adequate to describe the process by which Egdon Heath is generated by the text. When natural categories are fixed, one may speak about the ascription of human characteristics to inanimate beings or about the representation of an abstract or other impersonal entity in human terms. But Egdon is not so clear-cut; it is never given as entirely on one side of the animate/inanimate polarity before being assimilated to the other. Even in the opening chapter, the metaphoric expressions by which it is rendered human are immediately posited as literal (or as leading to liberal statements about the heath's role in human psychology): "Then [in storms, etc.] it became the home of strange phantoms, and it was found to be the hitherto unrecognized original of those wild regions of obsurity which are vaguely felt to be compassing us about in midnight dreams of flight and disaster, and are never thought of after the dream till revived by scenes like this" (bk. 1, chap. 1). Without drawing conclusions about Hardy's version of the unconscious, we find his prose moving from the metaphoric level (movement of storms || movement of phantoms), to statements that posit the heath as the original model of dream landscapes, to a final suggestion of its function as a permanent index of the unconscious "regions" of the mind itself. So steadily cummulative is this assimilation of the heath to the animate level that toward the close of the novel, as intensity of style mounts in tempo with intensity of action, we are prepared to take in stride such passages as this: "Skirting the pool [Eustacia] followed the path towards Rainbarrow, occasionally stumbling over twisted furze-roots, tufts of rushes, or oozing lumps of fleshy fungi, which at this season lay scattered about the heath like the rotten liver and lungs of some colossal animal" (bk. 5, chap. 7). While it is Eustacia who is stumbling toward her death, it is the heath that is seen here as a dismembered giant—neither clearly human nor, as Lawrence thought, merely bestial but a "colossal animal" who is martyred and distributed in a spectacular way.

While the interconnections of the animate and the inanimate must be deduced from the rhetorical modes of the opening chapter, later passages state their inherent identity in the heath with some urgency. The chief of these occurs in the first description of Eustacia Vye:

> There the form stood, motionless as the hill beneath. Above the plain rose the hill, above the hill rose the barrow, and above the barrow rose the figure. Above the figure was nothing that could be mapped elsewhere than on a celestial globe.
>
> Such a perfect, delicate, and necessary finish did the figure give to the dark pile of hills that it seemed to be the only obvious justification of their outline. Without it, there was the dome without the lantern; with it the architectural demands of the mass were satisfied. The scene was strangely homogeneous, in that the vale, the upland, the barrow, and the figure above it amounted only to unity. Looking at this or that member of the group was not observing a complete thing, but a fraction of a thing.
>
> (bk. 1, chap. 2)

Hardy employs the term "organic" in the next sentence to describe the internal relations of the "entire motionless structure"; we may apply it equally to the tenor of his thinking in this passage. Although the human figure is to be regarded aesthetically as a "necessary finish" and a satisfaction of an "architectural" demand, it is more fundamentally a "fraction" of a larger "unity." Or is the heath complete without the person: it needs it as its "obvious justification," to become a "homogeneous" being in its own right. The text speaks of this organic unity of the human and the nonhuman "members" of Egdon Heath as "a thing" and elsewhere adds, "a thing majestic without severity, impressive without showiness, emphatic in its admonitions, grand in its simplicity."

Although Eustacia is most striking in her unwilling assimilation into Egdon Heath, other characters exhibit a spectrum of possible relations to it, ranging from identification to detachment. Although the gigantic "thing" takes in both human beings and the heath, there are a number of possible modes of integration, which various characters explore. The peasants live in wary observance of the land and its seasons, but their limited mentalities are none too gently satirized in Hardy's folkish chapters. The reddleman, Diggory Venn, shows himself adroit not only in the world of commercial and (eventually) erotic competition but is especially competent among the highways and byways of the heath. (It is noteworthy that he gets no particular credit for this intimacy with the heath, as measured by the conventions of heroic stature; given Hardy's view of him as an "isolated and weird character"—in the "Author's Note" of 1912—he is scarcely ennobled by his numerous displays of omnicompetence.) It is Clym who displays the most complex relation to the heath, being the one who exercises a series of considered choices in the matter. In this first characterization, his constitution or generation by the place is stressed: "If any one knew the heath well it was Clym. He was permeated with its scenes, with its substance, and with its odours. He might be said to be its product" (bk. 3, chap. 2). At the end of his series of ideological shifts and personal misfortunes, he stands before the heath in an alien position, as of one face impervious to another: "there was only the imperturbable countenance of the heath, which, having defied the cataclysmal onsets of centuries, reduced to insignificance by its seamed and antique features the wildest turmoil of a single man" (bk. 5, chap. 2). But the most extreme separation from the heath—indistinguishable from a kind of rationalistic stupidity—is represented by the pragmatic objectivity of Thomasin Yeobright: "Egdon in the mass was no monster whatever, but impersonal open ground. Her fears of the place were rational, her dislikes of its worst mood reasonable" (bk. 5, chap. 8).

Despite their differences, the characters have a common connection with the heath, a unity of fate that is consistently figured in allusions to Prometheus: "Every night [the heath's] Titanic form seemed to await something; but it had waited thus, unmoved, during so many centuries, through the crises of so many things, that it could only be imagined to await one last crisis—the final overthrow" (bk. 1, chap. 1). The iconography of Prometheus chained to a mountain in the Caucasus is strikingly transmuted in this and similar passages: the *scene* of suffering becomes the sufferer (Egdon is not Caucasian but Titanic), while at least part of the demigod's character is ascribed to the land itself in its "unmoved" martyrdom. Yet the myth's primary orientation toward apocalypse (the final overthrow of Zeus) is, as we shall see, fully employed in *The Return*.

The heath's Promethean, long-suffering form of resistance is picked up in the characterization of the human actors but is resourcefully applied as a differentiating factor. The peasant's lighting of fires to celebrate Guy Fawkes Day, although localized as a modern British survival of the ritual death and rebirth of the year, is seen as the expression of a universal need: "Moreover to light a fire is the instinctive and resistant act of man when, at the winter ingress, the curfew is sounded throughout Nature. It indicates a spontaneous, Promethean rebelliousness against the fiat that this recurrent season shall bring foul times, cold darkness, misery and death. Black chaos comes, and the fettered gods of the earth say, Let there be light" (bk. 1, chap. 3). Here humans, heath, and Titans are seen on the same side, resisting—or at least protesting—an imposition from without, the fiat of a being or realm representing black chaos, winter, and death. Humanity joins with the land itself in "Promethean rebelliousness," and it is with one voice that they register their counterfiat; theirs is the voice of the "fettered gods" or Titans, which proclaims light—a biblical equivalent for the Promethean fire that is the subject of this passage.

The chief characters are, however, subtly distinguished in their articulations of this rebellion and thus in their associations with the band of "fettered gods." Eustacia is described from the first in terms derived from the preceding passage: "Egdon was her Hades, and since coming there she had imbibed much of what was dark in its tone, though inwardly and eternally unreconciled thereto. Her appearance accorded well with this smouldering rebelliousness. . . . A true Tartarean dignity sat upon her brow" (bk. 1, chap. 7). The term found in both passages, "rebelliousness," is linked to its consequences of banishment or living burial, whether of humans in Hades or of Titans in Tartarus (the variability of mythological traditions is exploited here to make these roughly equivalent terms for confinement in the earth). It is notable that this passage begins by emphasizing Eustacia's unwilling bondage in Egdon, the setting of her unsatisfactory station in life, but it gradually identifies her with the heath insofar as the latter, too, is unreconciled to its bound condition under the fiat of the ruling gods.

Precisely the opposite shift occurs in the course of Clym's characterization: beginning as one fully at home on the heath—"its product"—he becomes so thoroughly acclimated in his return to the soil that he renounces rebelliousness: "Now, don't you suppose, my inexperienced girl, that I cannot rebel, in high Promethean fashion, against the gods and fate as well as you. I have felt more steam and smoke of that sort than you have ever heard of. But the more I see of life the more do I perceive that there is nothing particularly great in its greatest walks, and therefore nothing particularly small in mine of furze-cutting" (bk. 4, chap. 2). Clym's liberal renunciation of the Promethean stance is part of an explicit cultural theme in the novel, concerned with the vulnerability of the modern mind by virtue of its skeptical intelligence, its loss of traditional, organizing mythologies (a loss and a vulnerability in which Hardy felt himself implicated). But Clym's career also involves a break with the creaturely tendency to rebellion against earthbound suffering, a separation from the Titanic "fettered gods" with whom Eustacia, involuntarily, associates herself. And it is this loss of Promethean vision that is his true undoing, for he sees "nothing particularly great in [life's] greatest walks" or, by the same token in the heath's.

Having detected the signs of a giant figure buried in the verbal integument of *The Return,* noted its provenance in Hardy's imaginings of his native place, and considered its shadowy relations with the characters of the drama, what can we say of the wider significance of this massive presence? The range of relevant contexts extends to the margins of the human imagination, for giants have populated not only folk and fairy tales, cosmogonies and epics, but also topographical prominences the world over. It is evident that Hardy would have known the Greek versions of this mythology, as well as its variants among the English romantic poets; it is perhaps less known that he was attentive to local legends accounting for curious outcroppings by tales of giants buried or sleeping in the land. Hardy recorded one such topographical fable in his notebook:

> The Legend of the Cerne Giant. He threatened to descend upon Cerne and to ravish all the young maidens on a particular night and to kill the young men next day. Goaded to desperate courage they waylaid and killed him, afterwards cutting his effigy on the hill. He lived somewhere up in the hills, was waited on by wild animals and used to steal the farmers' sheep, eating one a day. The *Giant's Head Inn* nearby evidently related to the tradition.

This explanatory tale registers what may be called the subdued-ogre variant of topographical gigantism but, as this is only one in a range of possibilities, a brief review of the alternatives will suggest a need for closer inspection if we are to single out the special face of Egdon Heath.

In contrast to the subdued ogre, the Titan lore with which Egdon Heath is associated stands in a tradition of proto-or prohuman giants reaching back to classical myth and descending to Hardy by way of Aeschylus and Shelley. Unlike the dead and buried giant whose form is left in the shape of hills or in markings upon them, the bound and tortured colossus of the Promethean strain is often placed within caves or in the rock face—

the better to express his continued protests in the form of rumblings, quakes, and other seismic phenomena. While the subdued ogre testifies to past victories by humanity, or at least by the local inhabitants, the bound Titan testifies to the present dominance of inimical powers and encourages continued but passive resistance to them. Hardy stands with his poetic master Shelley in removing the Titanic will from Aeschylus's mythic drama—making outspoken resistance like Eustacia's futile while establishing Egdon Heath as a figure of patient though brooding endurance.

A further extension of this long-suffering martyr to earthbound existence lies in a train of apocalyptic heroes of folk tales and legendary history around the earth. This figure is known to the Aarne-Thompson motif index under the rubrics "Culture hero still lives," "Culture hero asleep in mountain," and "Culture hero's expected return." Examples may be drawn from history (Charlemagne asleep within the Unterberg), religion (Balder and a host of other deities), or a mixture of history and myth (Arthur being the foremost example, one who is at home in the west of England). Neither dead and buried nor bound and rumbling, the culture hero looks to the promised future, and his legends partake of a popular apocalyptic impulse independent of religious eschatology. Common to these figures is their human scale, although invested with supernatural graces, they avoid the grotesquerie of gigantic expansion. Yet they are akin to the buried giants in their generalized potentiality; it is man himself who lies sleeping but latently liberated in these tales. Moreover, in some of his most spectacular variants, this sleeping savior is localized not merely under a hill or at a place but within an entire landscape; as Blake's Albion is the incarnation not merely of a national leader but of the land itself and the race's destiny.

Beyond Hardy's interest in topographical legends and primordial rituals, he was inevitably exposed to giant figures in the course of his lifelong absorption in the romantic poets. It is well known that he considered Shelley "our most marvellous lyrist" and quoted or alluded to his work perhaps more often than to any other, barring the Bible and Shakespeare. Although he devoted lavish encomiums to several favorite lyrics, Hardy clearly found *Prometheus Unbound* more to his fictional purpose. While it is relatively unrewarding to retrace the specific transactions with that epic-drama in *The Return's* Promethean imagery, there are important elements of Shelley's poetic mythology in Hardy's world view. Most striking in the action of both poem and novel is the appearance of the earth itself as a force in human destiny: for Shelley, this force is associated with the mysterious role of the earth-dwelling giant, Demogorgon, while for Hardy it is localized in Egdon Heath. The two are not the same, nor do they entail fully commensurate ideas of fate or necessity, but they are individualized figures of natural power abiding in the earth, with enormous regenerative potential. Indeed, the ambivalent reactions of awe and fascination generated by Demogorgon's gross majesty are akin to those inspired by Egdon's characterization.

Even more may be suggested, if without perfect assurance: the prescientific geological theories which have been shown to be at work behind Shelley's phrase "the breathing earth," as well as other references to animate underground expressions of the human condition, may have a place in the substructure of Hardy's setting. Earl Wasserman's studies of the poem's complex imagery of volcanism, earthquakes, and other geological processes reveal an ambiguity in Shelley's use of the figure which is matched in Hardy: "the single dominant image of the breathing earth symbolizes such opposite values as the volcanic disordering of the earth by Prometheus' curse and enchainment and also the revolutionary eruption that removes Jupiter. . . . volcanoes are catastrophic, but they also can stir the lethargic earth to action and to new forms." This mixture of rocklike, impervious, but restive power, subdued to long endurance yet rancourous in its arrested potentiality—along with quirky manifestations of smoldering hostility and a threat of direr disturbances—makes up the heroic stature of Shelley's earth demon and Hardy's heath. In both writers, the pathetic and the promising elements of the human condition are attached to the figures of giants; for Shelley, Prometheus and Demogorgon convey humanity's spiritual bondage and potential liberation; for Hardy, Egdon Heath combines the exhalations of age-old suffering and the expectancy of long-looked-for awakening: "The sombre stretch of rounds and hollows seemed to rise and meet the evening gloom in pure sympathy, the heath exhaling darkness as rapidly as the heavens precipitated it. . . . The place became full of a watchful intentness now; for when other things sank brooding to sleep the heath appeared slowly to awake and listen"(bk. 1, chap. 1).

The common fund of traditional lore for both conceptions lies in the classical mythology and localized legends of the Titans. Whether associated with Prometheus or Demogorgon, whether connected with volcanoes and earthquakes or the formation of islands and mountain ranges, the Titans play a vigorous role both in romantic poetry and in Hardy's latter-day version of its themes. The long theomachy of the Olympians and the Titans is a malleable political paradigm and has been adapted to national interests far beyond its Greek source; most germane for English mythmakers is the exiling of the defeated deities not to subterranean Tartarus but to an Atlantic island. The inevitable association of one of their number, Atlas, not only with the lost island of Atlantis but also with the British Isles provides abundant opportunities for the poets to connect the origins of Britain with a primal act of cultural rebellion, an exiled condition, and a foretold apocalypse.

Blake was well informed of such imaginative possibilities and, while Hardy's involvement with Blake has yet to be adequately assessed, it is clear that his sense of Titanic powers at work and at rest beneath the soil of England is matched only by Blake's among the English poets. While Hardy carefully selects the Titanic features of his landscape—seeing, e.g., Rainbarrow as a "wart on an Atlantean brow" (bk. 1, chap. 2)—Blake works out the features of his Albion in spectacular detail:

> London is between his knees, its basements fourfold;
> His right foot stretches to the sea on Dover cliffs, his heel
> On Canterbury's ruins; his right hand covers lofty Wales,
> His left Scotland;
> . . . .
> He views Jerusalem & Babylon, his tears flow down.
> He mov'd his right foot to Cornwall, his left to the Rocks of
> Bognor.
> He strove to rise to walk into the Deep, but strength failing
> Forbad, & down with dreadful groans he sunk upon his
> Couch
> In moony Beulah.

Lest there be any doubt about Blake's identification of Albion with a Titanic source, he makes this point explicit in the "Descriptive Catalogue" to his paintings, with regard to the lost "Ancient Britons": "The giant Albion, was Patriarch of the Atlantic; he is the Atlas of the Greeks, one of those the Greeks called Titans." And again in "A Vision of the Last Judgment": "He is Albion, our Ancestor, patriarch of the Atlantic Continent, whose History Preceded that of the Hebrews & in whose Sleep, or Chaos, Creation began." The generation of Blake's ideas from among the syncretic mythographers and their complex developments in the fabric of his poetry are matters to be followed up in other commentaries." But we can see in his poetic mythology and Hardy's a common concern to identify the sources not only of the present nation but of the land itself with a Titanic giant whose traces still lie open to inspection in the formations of the soil of England.

What emerges from these poetic and fictional versions of Britain's antediluvian history is a pattern of original settlement by gigantic creatures, following defeat and exile; their withdrawal, whether from renewed defeat or other calamity, into the earth (a significant variation on most myths of chthonic ancestors, who emerge *from* the native soil); and their dormant persistence under the feet of the present inhabitants, while awaiting a threatened cataclysm and possible restoration. Although human fate is inextricably bound up with the primal structures of the land and its speculative inhabitants, their restoration has no simple issue; the rising of the sleeping giants by no means guarantees a permanent liberation from their common oppression—and may portend the opposite. Thus Blake names one of the sons of Albion as Hylé (Greek for primal matter) and identifies him with Gog, taken in the biblical sense of the baser form of man. Though *Jerusalem's* climactic awakening of the sleeping giant, Albion, redeems all his sons in a general easement, the term Gog is again used to suggest that the terrible aspect of humanity's gigantism can never finally be put down. As [Northrop] Frye explains, "if behind the Bible there is the memory of an age of murderous ogres who perished in a stench of burning flesh, then in front of it there is an apprehension of a returning power of gigantic self-destruction. The former survives in the Bible as the Covering Cherub; the latter is portrayed as the giants Gog and Magog who return with the full power of darkness after the millennium."

Sifting through his web of folklore—both popular and poetic, markedly British and within Hardy's favorite range of reading—which of the strains of gigantism can be found uppermost in *The Return?* It is clear that the first type, the subdued ogre, is furthest from prominence, although Egdon has its baleful features; Hardy is least interested in celebrating humanity's past triumphs over chthonic powers in nature, for his view of both emphasizes their unity. The bound Titan, on the other hand, is the figure most obvious in the language of the text, and it seems evident that Hardy establishes in the Titanic heath the burden of a mankind forced to submit to an order of things that can only be explained (if it can be explained at all) as deriving from an arbitrary, if not a malevolent, authority. Yet space should be made for the third type of giant, not so much rebellious as long-suffering, dormant but expectant, who is implicated in the common fate of man and nature yet looks forward to an ultimate liberation.

In transforming *The Return* from the "ballad and pastoral romance" elements of its "Ur-novel," Hardy was applying to a more profound level of folklore, where reside the popular imaginings of origin, authority, and apocalypse which are given scope in giant lore. And, in effecting a "classical transvaluation" into the tragic mode, Hardy was drawing on a potentiality in Aeschylus which inspired Shelley, perhaps too avidly, in his *Prometheus*: the opening to the future which inspires hope. Egdon Heath carries, among its many resonances of power and endurance, a vibration not so much stoical as regenerative and creative—whatever the failures of its denizens to make much of their connections with it. This potentiality need not be—indeed resists being—specifically tied to historical events, either past revolutions or future ones. In underscoring the action of *The Return* with traces of apocalyptic promise, Hardy adds to a long tradition of English poetic figures—from Blake's, to Yeats's Rocky Face and Thomas's White Giant, who mark the intimations of aeonian change in the contours of the land.

Pastoralism and Modernity

Bruce Johnson

Far more important than the much analyzed classically tragic form of *The Return of the Native* (a form which has the single conspicuous flaw that it does not work very well) is its predictable return to the great intuitions of *Far from the Madding Crowd*. Clym, even though his "newness" was apparently not prominent in Hardy's mind during the first drafts of the manuscript, has come home seeking a nature consonant with his modern deracination, abulia, and melancholy. Further, if one comes to the novel fresh from the brilliantly recast pastoralism of *Far from the Madding Crowd*, the magnificent first chapter describing the heath is more calculated than has been apparent to most readers. For one thing, it is obviously Hardy's modern pastoral.

So we must anticipate that it will be a new, modern "native" who returns to Egdon Heath and that the heath is initially described with the emotional requirements of such a modern spirit in mind. Thus Egdon seems timeless, "a face on which time makes but little impression" (to quote the title of the first chapter) and reminds one immediately of those horizon-collapsing images usually associated with Fanny Robin in the previous novel. We are told that the only way to discover this "true tale" of the heath was to see it at dusk and just before dawn, when its "somber stretch of rounds and hollows seemed to rise and meet the evening gloom in pure sympathy." "And so the obscurity in the air and the obscurity in the land closed together in a black fraternization towards which each advanced half-

From *True Correspondence: A Phenomenology of Thomas Hardy's Novels*. University Presses of Florida, 1983.

way." The distinction between sky and land is collapsed in a manner far more significant than that suggested by mere nightfall: this almost sexual union between heath and night is its "true tale," its most essential nature. And that essence is phenomenologically associated with the similar horizon-collapsing images we have already discussed [elsewhere].

The connection between the heath image and those surrounding Fanny's visit to Troy's barracks and her coffin's journey home introduces us to a rather seminal ontological level of Hardy's feelings about these matters. If, as I have argued [elsewhere] those images suggest a failure of relation, we had better locate the qualities that are somehow collapsed or joined in sexual union in this short chapter. Oddly enough, the answer becomes rather simple when we recognize the central paradox of these introductory pages: that although the austere heath is precisely the landscape that must appeal to a mind obsessed with "the irrepressible New," and is a landscape suggesting precisely through that untragic austerity the new sense of an indifferent cosmos replacing outworn ideals of both classical and romantic beauty, the heath is also the most permanent, inviolate, ancient, obscure, obsolete, superseded, slighted and enduring, untamable, and primitive thing under the sun. Even the remnants of an ancient highway and barrow have been "almost crystallized to natural products by long continuance." Although the text suggests that the relation between "the irrepressible New" and the irrespressibly ancient is that the unaltering heath would give "ballast to the mind adrift on change, and harassed by the irrepressible New," we have come to recognize that these "collapsing" images are more threatening than that—that they disturb Hardy on a far less rational level than "ballast" would suggest.

Of course the affinity between night and the heath is not precisely the loss of all distinction that characterizes so ominously Fanny's call on Troy. Nevertheless the union of the heath with its "near relation" breeds obscurity and more obscurity. The human remains "crystallize" into something almost inseparable from the heath itself. If the heath is to provide ballast for the harassed new mentality, the more dominant image suggests that the *uralt* and the new are somehow lost in each other, that the key to the new is to be found in a new way of penetrating to the meaning of not just the old but of the most primitive, the unchanging beyond even the seeming permanence of landscape. Hardy carefully makes the point that Egdon is perfectly adapted for survival (in a very Darwinian way): "Those surfaces were neither so steep as to be destructible by weather, nor so flat as to be the victim of floods and deposits." The "last geological change" has only managed slight "finger-touches." Hardy has been reflecting on the geology of the heath in a very phenomenological manner, adducing the essence of its permanence as a kind of infinitely modulating quality, in contrast to the emotions of some of its inhabitants and to the great, tragic heath of Emily Brontë's Cathy and Heathcliff. It is a mistake to see the heath as some kind of topographical equivalent for the tragedy in this story. On the contrary, tragedy has an intrinsic involvement with time and timing, while the heath seems almost to have escaped time and offers an emotion for the modern sensibility that Hardy at this point can scarcely name, save that it is beyond tragedy. On the whole, then, it is curious that Hardy should have so loaded this novel with parallels to classical tragedy, when at the outset we are encouraged to pass beyond.

In sensing that the antidote to the ache of modernism lies in understanding the past in a new way, Hardy was very much aligned with the anthropology, geology, and psychology of his day, if not slightly in advance of it. Perhaps the most revolutionary discovery, made slowly during the entire nineteenth century, was that man and the earth were far, far older than anyone had imagined. If one even entertained the possibility that Darwin was right, the almost unimaginable stretch of time necessary for natural selection to produce species demanded an entirely new state of mind. The scale of things had changed. One has the feeling even while watching Milton contemplate the immensities of the creation of the universe that nonetheless his mind had not been stretched in the manner required of Hardy, Conrad, Tennyson, R. L. Stevenson, and other late Victorians. Once out of Milton's timeless heaven and potentially timeless Eden, the biblical history, however ancient, begins at once and at a rapid pace. We are not required to imagine the eons of warm seas which were man's most ancient home. It is one thing to imagine a God who always was, and quite another to imagine a man so old that as he recedes into the past he loses his identity among "lower" forms of life. It is stretching an argument only slightly to say that one of the newest things in the nineteenth century was the paleontological and geological past that had been so agonizingly uncovered.

Thus in this first chapter the primordial heath is less a possible ballast for the returning Clym's modern anguish than it is a modern and melancholy Walden, offering not transcendentalism but an acute immanentism; the meaning of the modern is found in its continuities with a past that was unimaginable before Lyell and Darwin. Clym returns, as he himself says, to rediscover what is essential in life and to strip away the very luxuries of life, thought, and feeling that Eustacia longs for with all her heart. In this surgical procedure the heath will eventually speak to him not of the difference between "the irrepressible New" and the past but of their identity. The true story of the heath is of the collapse of this particular distinction.

That Hardy is thinking in terms of the time span suggested by evolutionary processes (and by the unique quality this gives the remote past) is suggested by his description of the reddleman early in the second chapter as "of a class rapidly becoming extinct in Wessex, filling at present in the rural world the place which during the last century, the dodo occupied in the world of animals. He is a curious, interesting, and nearly perished link between the obsolete forms of life and those which generally prevail." The reddleman has chosen this profession almost perversely, and perhaps with some intuitive desire to be, if only for a few years, the kind of link Hardy mentions. Diggory is archaic in his determined loyalty and willingness to play the nemesis to those who deserve it. He will step into the modern world, but reluctantly and not yet.

It is Hardy's own mention of the forms of life "which generally prevail" that stimulates thoughts of the heath as a preeminently well-adapted creature, largely through the slow, quiet doggedness of its existence. Insofar as Diggory is truly a creature of the heath, his mode of existence and that of the heath are similar. The heath lives with the "apparent repose of incredible slowness. A condition of healthy life so nearly resembling the torpor of death is a noticeable thing of its sort; to exhibit the inertness of the desert, and at the same time to be exercising powers akin to those of the meadow, and even of the forest, awakened in those who thought of it the attentiveness usually engendered by understatement and reserve." To live at this richly subdued pace is to live forever and to live without—presumably—tragedy. Great geological cataclysms are not for Egdon. Furthermore, the rather tedious insistence (for the last page and a half of the chapter) on the organic unity of the gently rising heights, the barrow, and the single figure standing atop all, may suggest that at least some forms of human existence are consonant and even sympathetic with the heath's special mode of existence. One feels, as elsewhere when Hardy portrays these anicent barrows and rings, that the "Celts" were to his way of thinking far more closely attuned to their surroundings than subsequent cultures. In his essay on the need for preserving Stonehenge, Hardy is aware that Salisbury plain has not always looked as open as it did in his own day, yet he is struck by the fine and unnameable appropriateness of the structures to the surroundings. Had Clym been able to absorb the heath's mode as the ancient Celts may have (their structures seem to "crystallize" naturally into the scene), he might not have loved Eustacia and the ache of his modernism might well have been healed by the slow, natural rhythms of a "creature" that has survived the eons. And he would not have been Clym.

Often the heath seems to suggest to Hardy the biological or botanical and geological analogue of a strangely altered classical otium—beyond it, perhaps: a stoical attitude that would be as well-adapted as the heath for survival. The otium which in Gabriel Oak would be a rich contentment, slow and natural in its unfolding, becomes in *The Return of the Native* an austere refusal of extremes, but survives as an identifiable otium nonetheless.

Eustacia is established as a genuine antithesis to the heath in all its related meanings. Where it is stoic, she is tragic; where it survives, she aspires to burn out with a great passion; where it ignores time, she likes to stare at the sand running out in her small hourglass; where its botany and geology all seem tuned to avoid great conflicts, she courts them perversely. The heath accommodates, Eustacia violates. The heath has preeminently adjusted to its place in nature, Eustacia refuses hers in society and delights in flaunting its conventions: on hated Sundays she does housework and hums Saturday-night ballads; "On Saturday nights she would frequently sing a psalm, and it was always on a weekday that she read the Bible, that she might be unoppressed with a sense of doing her duty." She sides with the Philistines in schoolyard battles and, in a sentence that must be one of the most amusing Hardy ever wrote, "wondered if Pontius Pilate were as handsome as he was frank and fair." Hardy summarizes her mind as forswearing "compromise" and adds that if we are philosophically attracted to such boldness, "it is apt to be dangerous to the commonwealth." He is speaking of various sorts of commonwealth (not merely the body politic) and invites extrapolation to the Darwinian concept of adaptation. Eustacia is preeminently nonadaptive, and in this she is "divine" in the manner of the capricious old gods. Pagan, Corfiote, with the lip curves of old Greek statues, given to fits of melancholy and great excitement and passion, she is born to die tragically as surely as the heath will survive stoically. She aspires to enter the great world, but more precisely she aspires to the Dionysian fulfillment of personality.

In this fundamental opposition between Eustacia and the heath we have one of the more interesting permutations of the otium / aspiring mind dichotomy, and the heath and Clym and Eustacia have a good deal to do with the old pastoral. Eustacia sees her drive for an all-consuming passion as a kind of "ambition" in the long tradition of the aspiring mind. She admonishes Wildeve (whose first name is appropriately Damon): "Damon, you have not acted well; you have sunk in my opinion. You have not valued my courtesy—the courtesy of a lady in loving you—who used to think of far more ambitious things." There should be no romantic confusion about Eustacia's motives: she is a very ambitious and aspiring woman. Clearly, having conceived this aspect of her character, Hardy had to alter Clym somewhat to make him less obviously the disillusioned philosopher returning for survival to the pastoral world and more nearly, to her eyes, the successful and fashionable, if slightly Byronic, denizen of the great world caught while slumming. It is to Hardy's credit that he could see raw ambition in so intensely romantic an aspiration without diminishing the force and tragedy of it.

There is in Eustacia a considerable inheritance from the degenerating tradition of sensibility. In the manner of Sue Bridehead, she reminds me less of Emma Bovary than of the "man of feeling" who contemplates with pleasure the fact that he is feeling, and with more intensity and finesse than the oridinary folk around him. When Wildeve assures Eustacia that he will never "wish" to desert her, she replies:

> "I do not thank you for that. I should hate it to be all smooth. Indeed, I think I like you to desert me a little once now and then. Love is the dismallest thing where the lover is quite honest. O, it is a shame to say so; but it is true!" She indulged in a little laugh. "My low spirits begin at the very idea. Don't you offer me tame love, or away you go!"

Even in her most distraught moments, there seems always to be an aesthetic distance between Eustacia's feelings and her consciousness of them. Like most suicides (or so psychologists tell us) she may want to see herself as a suicide almost as much as she wants to contemplate herself loving greatly. We must remember that throughout this interview with Wildeve, the reddleman is listening, unobserved because he has almost completely covered himself with heath turves. He has literally become part of the heath, while they affirm their "hate" for it and Eustacia argues that it is her "cross, my shame, and will be my death!" Its very mode of existence is antipathetic to hers: as the reddleman lifts the turves and watches the black figures of Eustacia and Wildeve against the sky, they appear "as two horns which the sluggish heath had put forth from its crown, like a mollusk, and had now again drawn in."

How entirely misleading to see Egdon heath as an echo of Emily Brontë's tortured and romantic landscape, as do many of us who remember it at a distance of ten or twenty years. The heath does not echo or underwrite the tragic aspiration of Eustacia but seems instead to negate them. It is "sluggish"—quite the slowly surviving nemesis, somewhat in the way that the reddleman is to the story, and much as his trade is, to use the anthropological term, a "survival." The mollusk image suggests that even these two, at least one of whom is a passionately aspiring "feeler," are ontologically subsumed by another order of existence. The heath endures at least partly because it is so archaically fundamental—beyond and beneath even the most intense human feelings and certainly beyond Eustacia's fine scrutiny of her feelings. It is as though Hardy is intimating that evolution has finally produced a creature who is too determinedly self-reflective and (in feelings riddled with self-consciousness) too artificial to survive. The mollusks survive, the heath survives, Diggory survives. All this artificiality in Eustacia, of course, calls into question the possibility of real tragedy for her. The old Greek tragic heroes did not avidly pursue their self-images as tragic heroes. They felt their tragedy immediately and without the intervention of an almost literary self-image: "In emotion she was all the while an epicure."

That Eustacia should use the ancient Rainbarrow and ceremonial fires as the trappings of her on-and-off romantic enthusiasm for Wildeve somehow fits her appropriation of the mummer's role as a means of catching a glimpse of Clym. In describing the mummers as a "survival," Hardy is using a word crucial to understanding his attitude toward the past. It is not irrelevant, then, that Eustacia is rather strangely described as having "the greatest contempt" for "mummers and mumming." Why "the greatest contempt"? No really adequate explanation is ever given, except that the mummers are part of the rustic isolation she feels on the heath, so that mumming and the heath are joined in her mind. More important, though Hardy never discusses the issue directly, is the obvious linking of the ancient mumming with the even more ancient survival qualities of the heath, the barrows, the ceremonial fires. Eustacia intuitively hates the mumming because it is involved with the mode of existence that apparently undercuts her own. And this is not alone to say that the stoic, accommodating toughness of the heath is opposed to her propensity for short-lived destructive tragedy: the heath and all other "survivals" in this novel contradict precisely the emotional epicureanism and artificiality of Eustacia. Though hard to recognize, she is a further refinement of the almost surreal artificiality that Clym has fled in Paris and the diamond business. She seeks out Clym not as a unique individual whom she will love because of what he is, but as a likely candidate for the role her imagination has created despite what he is, namely a man in love with the heath and the survivals and all they mean.

Hardy knows better than most how perfunctory many of these survivals are:

> A traditional pastime is to be distinguished from a mere revival in no more striking feature than this, that while in the revival

> all is excitement and fervour, the survival is carried on with a stolidity and absence of stir which sets one wondering why a thing that is done so perfunctorily should be kept up at all. Like Balaam and other unwilling prophets, the agents seem moved by an inner compulsion to say and do their allotted parts whether they will or no. This unweeting manner of performance is the true ring by which, in this refurbishing age, a fossilized survival may be known from a spurious reproduction.

I quote this passage at length because it is one of the most likely to be misread in the entire novel. Hardy is not gently satirizing those who numbly continue those traditions and suggesting that such things may as well be dropped. The word "fossilized" is invariably misleading to a reader who has not begun to recapture the excitement that fossils created in the nineteenth century. Of course the whole passage is laced together with irony, but the "stolidity" with which the "survival" is presented is sterility only to the unsympathetic viewer. In fact Hardy's irony throughout is designed to capture the urbane scepticism of one of the creatures of the "refurbishing age."

But this "stolidity and absence of stir" with which the mummers perform suggests something of the survival quality of the heath, the barrows, the fires, and the mumming itself. Like the May "walking" which opens *Tess of the D'Urbervilles,* these ceremonies contain a power that survives the perfunctoriness that modern man often unconsciously uses to disguise their frightening significance. If competition in decorating the costumes leaves Saint George looking pretty much like the "deadly enemy," the Saracen, it is Hardy who reminds us of the archaic meaning by having the "pagan" Eustacia play the Turkish Knight. Eustacia is antithetical to all the potentially deep continuity represented by these survivals, however disguised and distorted they may have become. Hardy had for them a tremendous respect that far transcends any notion of mere nostalgia and probably went far deeper into his major aesthetic concerns than even he could articulate. If the great signal fires of the autumnal equinox, with, as Hardy says, all their Promethean meaning and their role in the profound cycles of birth and death and rebirth, are today disguised by some ersatz association with the Powder Plot, the feelings and actions which these fires precipitate have no difficulty blending harmoniously with the lives of those who built the great barrow and the bonfires of the past.

When Eustacia, however, plays the Turkish Knight, she rants the words with only a superficial resemblance to the way the role is usually played. "Like in form, it had the added softness and finish of a Raffaelle after Perugino, which, while faithfully reproducing the original subject, entirely distances the original art." Eustacia stands against the meaning of the heath and of the "survivals" largely because she characteristically has this refining, epicurean, overcivilizing if antisocial quality to her every thought and action. Of course Raphael studied and imitated Perugino (one recalls Berenson's comment, "At whose feet did he not sit?"). But Raphael almost immediately refines away the utterly pristine, pastoral elegance of a Perugino.

The "ranting" of the mummers is a truly primitive, compulsive prophecy, coming in all its rote and outward stolidity from the most fundamental wellsprings of European experience: the Western tradition challenged by an alien culture, light by darkness. The mummers do not understand this, they transmit it. Eustacia's intuitive refining and softening of the whole performance is precisely the only thing in the performance with the unmistakable hint of denial in it. The mummery has survived in a manner reminiscent of the heath's: it has been able to accommodate all the fancy costumes and blurring of characters without losing its basic identity. Can there be any doubt, however, that the coming of people such as Eustacia is the beginning of the end? Her refining "entirely distances the original art," as a Raphael does the pristine Perugino. It is the same aesthetic distance that we find lying ominously between her feelings and her consciousness of them. The decadence is truly that seen so exaggeratedly in the "man of feeling" and in the decline of the tradition of sensibility. The supreme irony is that the only man who can see the importance of these survivals (as he does of the heath-life) and possibly interpret them as some kind of priest-philosopher, is precisely the man she now hunts for the lead role in her romantic passion.

I do not mean to cast Eustacia as some ultimate in decadent sophistication. Quite the contrary, she is in many ways entirely naive, and Clym is supposed to be the world-weary sophisticate. Her role in quickly seeing to it that Wildeve marries Thomasin is, however, anything but ingenuous and must rank with other high points of cynical opportunism in the English novel. The reddleman is the only innocent person in the entire affair, coldly used by all concerned, even Thomasin herself. Eustacia's naiveté is an elusive quality hard to attribute to any one of her characteristics and yet most intimately associated with her pervasive faith in the satisfaction to be had through great passion. She is innocent of the knowledge that causes definitively modern melancholy in Clym, that makes his worn face the new standard of beauty, "the typical countenance of the future." She at least has an innocent faith in the efficacy of *some* kind of human emotion.

It is not in Eustacia's dread of the heath that this novel gives us great symbolic difficulty but in Clym's love for it. The paradox is simply this: he is the true child of the heath ("permeated with its scene, with its substance, and with its odors. He might be said to be its product"); yet he is also Hardy's embodiment, in this novel, of all that is modern. Even his childhood toys had been "the flint knives and arrowheads which he found there, wondering why stones should 'grow' to such odd shapes." To many, Hardy says, "this Egdon was a place which had slipped out of its century generations ago, to intrude as an uncouth object into this. It was an obsolete thing, and few cared to study it." It is, in short, another of the "survivals" that so interest Hardy. Our paradox, more precisely, is that anyone so entirely modern as Clym should also be the very child of this ancient thing and react with "barbarous satisfaction" at seeing some of the attempts to farm the heath fail. If Clym, sickened and disillusioned at the modern life he has seen, were returning to the heath for all its ancient survival values, we should understand at once. But, strangely enough, Clym's modernity and his identity as a true child of the ancient heath seem to be very similar in Hardy's mind. Clym may return to the essentials of rustic life and heath-existence in flight from the "idlest, vainest, most effeminate business that ever a man could be put to," but there is nothing in the heath that can cure the anguish of his modernity. In a very surprising sense, Clym's intimate knowledge of the heath and its meaning serves to *confirm* the assorted knowledge that constitutes his modernity. Ancient and modern are conflated, *if* we appreciate that in the heath the idea of the past has been given a new dimension by Hardy.

As the sensate being that Hardy's imagery continually makes it, the heath "knows" the "defects of natural laws," that brilliantly succinct phrase that sums up so much of the late-Victorian predicament; and the heath survives by its own "wild and ascetic" ways, the key to the whole pattern of survival being ascetic and yet strategic endurance. Both the heath and Clym are definitively ascetic and understated. As he tells his mother when she asks him why he cannot accept a life of self-indulgence as well as others can:

> "I don't know, except that there are many things other people care for which I don't; and that's partly why I think I ought to do this. For one thing, my body does not require much of me. Well, I ought to turn that defect to advantage, and being able to do without what other people require I can spend what such things cost upon anybody else."

This is an ascetic faith that, except for its spirit of sacrifice, might almost be the motto of the heath as a geological and biological entity. After all, the phrase "wild and ascetic" that I used above was evoked by Hardy to describe the young Clym, but in a context that makes it clear his peculiar kind of wildness and asceticism are heath-born. To complete another of the contrasts that lie at the core of this tragedy, we need only remember that Eustacia is a peculiarly self-indulgent woman in the manner of decadent sensibility that I have outlined. The apparent austerity of the heath, as much as its loneliness and wildness, is what alienates her.

Yet the slow, even sluggish asceticism of the heath and Clym is possibly the way to cope with the knowledge they both seem to have of existence. As a survival, the heath reveals the means of its survival, and two of its ancient artifacts are made to bear the modern flower, the emblem itself of the ability to survive toughly on almost nothing: "The only visible articles in the room [Eustacia's] were those on the window-sill, which showed their shapes against the low sky: the middle article being the old hour-glass, and the other two a pair of ancient British urns which had been dug from a barrow near, and were used as flower-pots for two razor-leaved cactuses." This is one of the most powerful images in the entire novel, the hourglass having been used earlier to signal Eustacia's impatience with time in contrast to the slow, almost timeless quality that Hardy invariably associates with the sheer stamina of survivals.

That these "razor-leaved cactuses" should grow in the urns, the ancient British urns, suggests a distinction in Hardy's mind between the usefulness for the modern British sensibility of the Hellenic past and the native, British past. The Hellenic is dead:

> The truth seems to be that a long line of disillusive centuries has permanently displaced the Hellenic idea of life, or whatever it may be called. What the Greeks only suspected we know well; what their Aeschylus imagined our nursery children feel. The old-fashioned reveling in the general situation grows less and less possible as we uncover the defect of natural laws, and see the quandary that man is in by their operation.

Even the Hellenic ideal of beauty has lost relevance. Hardy contends that "the view of life as a thing to be put up with" has replaced "that zest for existence which was so intense in early civilizations," all of which may suggest an irony in these cactuses growing from the urns (albeit that they are probably funerary) of a presumably zestful earlier civilization. The persistent reference to the consonance of the early British barrows and remains with the heath itself, however, would suggest that while the Roman legions hurried to be clear of Egdon by November, fearing its dismal ambience, there were natives who understood and built their barrows in such a way that they seemed the natural culmination of the scene. Clym is the direct heir of these earlier natives.

If one is uncomfortable in pursuing the close resemblance of Clym and the heath it is probably because some critics have made much of the fact that while the heath presents a face unaffected by time, Clym's face is "modern" precisely because it is so thoroughly and symbolically the record of his disillusionment. Such observations ignore, however, the early reference to "haggard Egdon" and Hardy's claim that "like man" the heath is "slighted and enduring." The heath is "obscure, obsolete" and "superseded." Clearly Hardy meant to imply that Clym's modern knowledge consists primarily in realizing not only that neither the universe nor its laws were made for man but that man feels slighted by whatever universal plan may emerge from the discoveries of modern science. Man is a "survival," as the heath, mummery, and November Fifth bonfires are.

And like the mummery, for example, he possesses a potential power that far transcends the apparent rote of his existence. Just as the power of the May walking in *Tess of the D'Urbervilles* or the fires or mummery in *The Return of the Native* can be released by probing their incredible antiquity, so man by beginning to discover his antiquity may release an unheard-of potential within himself. But of course the antiquity that must be approached is unlike anything that any century before the nineteenth knew about. Now we are in a position to understand why Hardy should have reported that his blood ran cold when the Maumbury Ring was discovered to have paleolithic origins. If in probing the most remote origins of "St. George and the Dragon" the anthropologically minded can discover primitive rituals concerning the birth, death, and rebirth of the seasons, so man in his capacity as a survival (slighted, enduring, obscure, and obsolete) can probe within himself for an analogous meaning.

This quality of being slighted and regarded as obsolete is at the roots of Hardy's respect and sympathy for the literally hundreds of survivals he records so lovingly in his novels and poems. Like them, man exists a seeming stranger in the new universe that Victorian science had made—somewhat old-fashioned, enigmatic, but above all carrying a runic message to be read only by those who sense its far from superseded power. It is no exaggeration to say that all Hardy's art comes around eventually to the problem of understanding man against the background of antiquity that had earlier in the century made biblical accounts of creation and genealogy seem like yesterday, and that always for Hardy made Roman England seem the very top of that blood-chilling excavation to man's origins. When Clym tells Eustacia that there is "a very curious Druidical stone" on the heath and assumes she must often go to see it, she replies that she knows of no such stone: "I am aware that there are Boulevards in Paris." They separate a moment later, and Hardy says that under the prospect of their coming great passion, "her past was a blank, her life had begun." Her "blank" past, in contrast with Clym's desire to read the runic meaning of man's survival, to possess a past so vast and symbolic that we are still struggling with its emotional impact one hundred years later, provides the true conflict and tragedy of this novel. Eustacia is not only a lover but his nemesis on this most important issue of his life.

Hardy's intuitive identification of man himself as a survival, in the most far-reaching late-nineteenth-century sense of that word, is a metaphor of incalculable importance. It destroys at once any notion that Hardy's taste for these rustic ceremonies, words, and customs was merely nostalgia or an attempt to live a moment longer in a pastoral world far from perfect but infinitely preferable to the one aborning. It explodes any notion of the heath as Sartrean "in-itself" and Clym and Eustacia as somehow tragically fated "for-itself" consciousness, finally confronted with the ultimate nemesis of indifferent matter. If both the heath and man are survivals, the description of them as Ishmaelitish grows in importance.

It is the fate of Ishmael (though only the son of Abraham and a slave) to be disinherited by Sarah for the benefit of her own son Isaac. The distance from Melville's "Call me Ishmael" to the Ishmaelitish heath and heath "native" is not so great as the gap of twenty-seven years and a world of American experience might suggest. The anthropological survival is by definition disinherited and cast into the wilderness of a foreign time, where it will not be understood and its runic message may become merely picturesque. If man in Hardy's eyes is also a survival, it is because he finds himself outliving the divinely ordered universe in which his place was primary. In the new universe, his longing for an ethical purpose to creation and for a meaningful role within it is outdated, obsolete, even quaint from some positivist perspectives. And like Ishmael, the new man finds himself in a wilderness specifically in having lost whatever favor or inheritance he might have had. The nineteenth-century Ishmael, be he Melville's or Hardy's, lies under the curse of being a wild man (as does the biblical figure) in the sense of needing to become a kind of philosophic hero who, cast out of one orderly world, must ask the most disruptive questions in order to make a new one.

In losing the inheritance and favor of an earlier world view (involving, no doubt, some Emersonian correspondence of appearance and reality), Melville's Ishmael must virtually go back to epistemological origins. There are no longer any guidelines for moving from the phenomenal to the noumenal world, nor any guarantee in the world of appearance that a noumenal world lies behind it at all. Even the idea that the world of the senses was somehow a product of the Fall (and thus that the senses were deceptive, misleading, and even the instruments of the devil) was a guarantee of noumenal reality to a good many Puritan sensibilities, who proceeded at their crudest to reverse the sense data in order to arrive at the real. I think it is possible to see that Hardy makes Clym a kind of would-be wild man not only in his taste for the most rudimentary heath-life but in his somewhat optimistic desire to reexamine the meanings of life in the most fundamental way.

It appears, however, that Hardy has once more given us some of the old pastoral spirit for grasping Clym's attempt to live in the wilderness of the new skepticism. After all, the implication of a survival is that it conceals an important meaning which can be evoked if we understand its original context. Thus, when Hardy remarks that the mumming of St. George ends with nobody commenting any more than they "would have commented on the fact of mushrooms coming in autumn or snowdrops in spring," he may be intimating that the survival just performed had almost the same level of significance as vegetative rebirth and cycle. Does it follow that man may be the only survival who bears no such important meaning, in the sense that the old context in which he had meaning is *absolutely* discredited (i.e., that an ethically and divinely ordered universe is simply a lie)?

The term "survival" was first used by E. B. Tylor in his 1871 *Primitive Culture,* a title which turns up in Hardy's *Literary Notes* while he summarizes a passage from Herbert Spencer. There is no hint that Hardy had read Tylor's earlier *Anahuas* or *Mexico and the Mexicans, Ancient and Modern* of 1861 or the more important *Researches into the Early History of Mankind and the Development of Civilization* of 1865, but the evidence of *The Return of the Native* suggests that he had almost certainly become familiar by the early 1870s with the importance of the concept of survivals to evolutionist method. As Tylor said in 1871,

> These are processes, customs, opinions and so forth which have been carried on by force of habit into a new state of society different from that in which they had their original home, and they thus remain as proofs and examples of an older condition of culture out of which a newer has been evolved.

Hardy may even have read or heard of John Lubbock's *The Origin of Civilization* (1870) or his earlier *Pre-Historic Times, as Illustrated by Ancient*

Remains and the Manners and Customs of Modern Savages (1865), since Lubbock was to my knowledge the only early evolutionary anthropologist who both pioneered the study of survivals and at great length claimed that Fetishism was the earliest stage of the evolution of religion, which then grew through Nature Worship, Shamanism, and Idolatry on to a modern conception of God as "the author, not merely a part, of nature." In trying to describe the complex November sound of the heath as the "united product of infinitesimal vegetable causes," of the wind entering the "mummied" heath bells, Hardy concludes:

> The spirit moved them. A meaning of the phrase forced itself upon the attention; and an emotional listener's fetichistic mood might have ended in one of more advanced quality. It was not, after all, that the left-hand expanse of old brooms spoke, or the right-hand, or those of the slope in front; but it was the single person of something else speaking through each at once.

This "evolution" is really an unmistakable period piece which could have been influenced by Tylor's description of the evolution of religion in *Primitive Culture* (1871) but, with its emphasis on fetishism as a distinct stage which we "advance" beyond, is more characteristic of Lubbock and would not again be entirely characteristic of another such theory until Frazer and *The Golden Bough* (1890) or *Totemism* (1887). Suffice it to say that Tylor's evolution of religious feeling is a far subtler theory that does not offer fetishism as a distinct stage at all. In fact, Hardy's passage seems to note rather precisely (and somewhat ironically) that moment when the mind seems to "progress" from seeing spirit *in* nature to feeling that some noumenal presence beyond nature is simply speaking through the various natural details of the heath. For Lubbock this was the most important moment in the evolution of religion, though he would have suggested three or four more stages between fetishism and any such realization.

Comte and Herber Spencer, though not exactly evolutionary anthropologists, were very much interested in fetishism as a stage in the development, the evolution, of their religion of mankind. Hardy's *Literary Notes* contains annotated passages from Comte and Spencer in which fetishism and the evolution of religious feeling are precisely the issue, although Spencer as we might expect is using his view of fetishism to attack the positivist position. There are uses of the term and the idea of fetishism often enough in *Tess of the D'Urbervilles* to suggest that if Hardy had discovered the word in translations of Comte, he thought of it in connection with that not unrelated evolutionary spirit infusing both things and people in that novel.

When Hardy's friend Frederic Harrison awkwardly suggested to Hardy that *Tess* "reads like a Positivist allegory or sermon," he had at least applied a popular term to Hardy's very personal tendency in the novel toward a form of synthesizing consciousness. . . . Although the "progress" and positivist method implicit in all Comte's writing was uncongenial to Hardy, the idea of a talismanic power inhering in things seemed to fascinate Hardy as some kind of access to man's deepest archaism. Elsewhere in the *Literary Notes* Hardy summarizes a passage from Herbert Spencer's *Principles of Biology* (1864), in which Spencer argues that "it cannot be said that inanimate things present no parallels to animate ones."

Whether it may be Lubbock or Comte or Spencer in the background here is relatively unimportant. Hardy is in any event demonstrating that he comes to *The Return of the Native* full of recent anthropological orientations and queries and that foremost in his mind is the issue of survivals so important to Tylor's *Primitive Culture.* We have at last, I think, an explanation for the crescendo of interest in survivals (including his use of the term itself) in this novel. Hardy had of course always been interested in old folkways, but in *The Return of the Native* he suddenly has a conceptual frame that both contributes to and extensively modifies the old pastoral ensemble of language and attitudes so important to *Far from the Madding Crowd.*

All through the 1860s and at least since Lewis Henry Morgan's *League of the Ho-de-no-sau-nee,* or *Iroquois* (1851), the idea of survivals had been part of the intellectual climate. H. S. Maine and J. F. McLennan had discussed the problem with regard to marriage (*Primitive Marriage,* 1865) and law (*Ancient Law,* 1861), and of course Darwin himself had provided biological models for the anthropological ploy in 1859. One is not to assume, however, that the biological model was fundamental in the discovery and use of survivals as an important part of the comparative method. Their prominence during this crucial period of 1851 through 1878 (to use the date of *The Return of the Native*) was undoubtedly due to changes in mental habits even more fundamental than those occasioned by Darwin—changes having to do with a dawning realization of the way the past could lie *in* the present and of the ultrabiblical antiquity of the past. No doubt the spirit of Lyell was equally moving in the *Literary Notes: "The enthusiasm* of Sir Charles Lyell, who when travelling along a cutting gazed out of the railway carriage as if the sides were hung with beautiful pictures."

Incredibly, then, not only the bonfires, the mumming, and so on, are survivals, but the heath and man himself are conceived of in this great anthropological vein. Survivals were used by these evolutionary anthropologists to reconstruct the antecedent stages of cultural evolution, and when such method came under attack by modern relativist anthropologists, it was by means of challenging the uselessness that men such as Tylor were alleged too have seen in survivals. A modern "functionalist" anthropologist would claim that in calling a particular activity a survival (and therefore functionless in its present context), Tylor and his followers had paid insufficient attention to the ways such apparently atrophied practices have assumed new and often subtle functions in the new culture. As Marvin Harris points out in his discussion of the problem, such attacks completely misrepresent the customary use of survivals by evolutionary anthropologists, who did not regard "uselessness" in the survivals' present context as an essential part of the definition.

Hardy, as he often does, anticipates this most subtle crux of modern anthropological method by intimating at considerable length that the ceremony of the fires, though its ancient religious or ritual context no longer holds, continues as the answer to some basic, human, Promethean need to defy the coming of winter's darkness as well as of some kind of psychic darkness. Indeed, Hardy characteristically refuses to see any of the hundreds of survivals that fill his novels (especially from *The Return of the Native* on) as defined by their being useless or purposeless in the present context. It is easy enough to see that they emerge from a time when their details would have had a ready explanation; but on the whole Hardy's point is that they survive, often if not invariably, because they reach a human need that transcends changes in culture, or at least all but the most seminal changes in culture. Hardy had apparently no great faith that some uniform evolutionary pattern would be discovered for culture, as it either had been or would be for biological man. Thus he is deliberately a bit facile when he mentions the "advance" from the fetishistic stage or when he uses some variation of Morgan's stages of savagery, barbarism, and civilization. But he is nonetheless willing, as few of his contemporary novelists were, to proceed from the evidence of survivals of all kinds to a diachronic sense of man's identity that far surpassed the most elaborate synchronic definitions of his day. Hardy was better than most at placing his characters in a rich, synchronic social context, even to the extent of relating neighborhoods to counties, districts, and regions; families to crossroads, towns, and cities; and so on in the manner demonstrated so brilliantly in Tess's endless walks and in his discussions of Casterbridge in *The Mayor of Casterbridge*. But it was to the past, largely through the whole concept of a survival, that Hardy turned, expecting to discover not the laws of culture's evolution but the qualities in man that survive the alteration of culture.

Clym and Hardy, however, part company on just this issue of what it is of inestimable value that the survivals may reveal. Fascinated as he is by the old folkways, when Eustacia is jabbed with a hat pin in church, Clym declares that he has "come to clear away those cobwebs," to educate the heath people away from their irrational superstitions. He would, on the whole, try to give them a rational view of their place in creation that would stoically equip them to bear the vale of tears. He says to Eustacia, "There is no use in hating people—if you hate anything you should hate what produced them." No doubt Clym means ignorance, superstition, and a generally irrational approach to life. Yet Eustacia answers him immediately with a comment that must represent the measure of Hardy's ironic distance from Clym: "Do you mean Nature? I hate her already." It has not occurred to Clym that Nature is in some sense the source of both the best qualities in the survivals *and* Susan Nunsuch's belief in witches.

If we follow the analysis of survivals back toward some primitive essence of man, rationality is not what we discover. Clym's "high thinking" seems to ignore the quality of his own intimate relationship with the heath. Though apparently Clym believes a kind of rational stoicism will prove the best survival quality he can offer the heath people, these "clowns" already survive pretty well with an irrationality which, if it produces superstition and Susan Nunsuch with her needle, has also produced in its symbiotic, even mythic and ritualistic capacity the continuity of the survivals themselves.

The great fires which begin the novel are the perfect example. They are important both to Hardy and the rustics who year after year create them for more than a moderately pleasant social event. They are as much "prophetic" and capable of affecting Hardy on an inarticulate, almost impersonal level as some of the survivals that were to fascinate Morgan, Tylor, Frazer, and finally a whole panoply of modern artists (and of these last, even some great ones could never entirely believe that Madam Sosostris's pack of cards was a dead and debased mystery to the modern world, or that those dried currants would never more speak of Dionysus and the fertility cults). The continuity with the past that would have been so sustaining to T. S. Eliot was not a rational matter so much as it was chthonic and spiritual. Eliot was able to involve Christianity in these other, more ancient ritual survivals; Hardy does not and did not even try. To the heath people, as to the rustics of *Far from the Madding Crowd,* Christianity is largely a social issue or the basis for rather comic discussions about high church and low church. Almost nobody manages to get to church in *The Return of the Native,* and when Eustacia finally does arrive she is immediately the victim of pagan superstition.

Hardy was never certain whether the lives of these heath people were really sustained to any degree by their involvement in the hundreds of pagan survivals that weave in and out of their existence. Surely they are more involved in the old pagan ways than in the Christian, but Hardy is never certain that he can attribute to the natives even an intuitive participation in the meaning of these survivals. *Meaning,* however, is a quasi-rational term that we need not impose on the obvious *involvement* of these people in the great symbolic cycles and rhythms of existence that make Clym's high thinking seem the most arrogant presumption.

In short, if we follow these survivals back to the earlier world view and "stage" of human culture that they imply, we recover not a *discredited* and now useless view of a noumenously significant Nature, but an original state of mind which, Hardy would like to say, has a truth of its own. The question is, can he bring himself to claim such a usefulness? He is trapped in a dilemma in which the "truth" of modern science seems to demand that, on one hand, we discredit the various ritualistic and mythic ways in which the natural world seems pregnant with human relevance, though, on the other, these great mythic meanings call to us as they called to T. S. Eliot and D. H. Lawrence and Yeats and Joyce. This ambivalence is rather nicely embodied in Hardy's attitude toward Clym's missionary zeal. He is both the child of the heath and the stepson of modern skepticism; sustained by his Antaeus-like dependence on the heath, he would yet bring to its inhabitants the gifts of his rationalism, a rationalism whose consequences have driven him back to the heath in the first place.

The stance Hardy is slowly working toward seems to involve the loss of a pride that demands of Nature more than man's equal participation in these great rhythms and sympathies. If rationalism and the heightened self-consciousness it encourages demand a natural world with a human ethical rationale, we shall be eternally and definitively frustrated—tragic or pathetic creatures depending on our degree of ego and presumption. If, on the contrary, we allow the survivals to help take us back to a time and state of mind where one does not feel the necessity of imposing human ethics on natural order, a certain kind of peace may be possible: and this peace may be the ultimate otium, the new otium consonant with the demands of the new pastoral. But Hardy's question is always whether such loss of pride, such peace, is really compatible with consciousness itself—whether it is not in the essence of consciousness, especially self-consciousness, to be always outside these rhythms and thus instinctively critical of them. A similar problem lies at the very core of D. H. Lawrence's best work.

It is, after all, one thing to be at peace—and nearly absorbed—by the Nature of the old pastoral and quite another to yield to a truly diachronic nature extending back and beyond the "carboniferous" age, where no birds sing and the soft ferns seem "machine-made foliage, a world of green triangles with saw-edges, and not a single flower." This famous passage is simply another one of those moments when the entire idea of the natural world is suddenly brutalized as much by a knowledge of the mechanics of evolution as by the sheer meaning of an incredibly extended antiquity. If we are to yield to the much earlier state of mind discussed above, will we not discover that this natural world is itself a kind of hidden mechanism that in its early, most revealing periods produced its true image in "machine-made foliage" with its ominous "saw-edges" and "monotonous extent of leafage": Hardy is infinitely attracted to this new otium yet deeply fearful that the natural world is not worthy of the sacrifice involved. Is the later Clym, nearly blind and so much a part of the heath that he is at times indistinguishable from it, a better man than the clear-sighted missionary of the novel's opening? Is it a question of man coming home (possibly through some of the survivals that had allowed the evolutionary anthropologists a conceptual point of entry they had previously lacked)? Or is it more nearly true to say that the fundamental myth is not the possibility of the return of the native but whatever myth would make man not a survival but a mutation, an Ishmaelitish creature whose essence is never to have been "native" anywhere at any time? *The Return of the Native* questions the viability not so much of the word *return* as of the word *native*.

That Hardy still views this larger dilemma in the context of otium and the aspiring mind is sufficiently emphasized by his continual reference to the ambition of Eustacia. Flinging himself upon the heath (actually the Rainbarrow itself), Clym watches the eclipse of the moon and waits for this prearranged signal to bring Eustacia. He longs to escape the aspiration of Eustacia and his mother in favor of a "world where personal ambition was not the only recognized form of progress—such, perhaps, as might have been the case at some time or other in the silvery globe then shining upon him."

As Clym goes on to contemplate the topography of the moon we realize that this is an important moment in the history of the pastoral: to escape the aspiring mind (Clym's missionary goals are rather selfless) apparently necessitates an imaginative flight to the moon. From one's own vineyard to Arcady to the moon, in slightly less than two thousand years! We must travel farther and farther to flee that ancient aspiring mind. He passionately views it for a few moments as a symbol of his much-sought peace and otium, and, of course, it is the eclipse of that moon which is the signal for Eustacia's arrival. Eustacia's aspirations extend even to the eclipse of that most remote fantasy of Clym's peace. The symbolism is a bit heavy, but unmistakable. The shadow "widens" until Eustacia (whose grandfather was characteristically epic, "a sort of Greek Ulysses"), falls into his arms. Her love will be the death of his dream of otium, or the total eclipse of it. We really do not know which is the more intense of Eustacia's aspirations, her taste for the great world of luxury ("luxurious" is Clym's description) or for the all-consuming passion of a great love in which marriage is the ultimate boredom. Most basically understood, she aspires to seeing herself in a great love from the luxurious aesthetic distance we discussed earlier.

As Eustacia seduces him from his asceticism and dream of pastoral peace, the eclipse progresses until she says: "Clym, the eclipsed moonlight shines upon your face with a strange foreign color, and shows its shape as if it were cut out in gold. That means that you should be doing better things than this." The "gold" is symbolically consonant with the meaning the scene has established for the eclipsed moon, the eclipse by her ambition of his pastoral dream ("I could live and die in a hermitage here, with proper work to do").

After the conversation in which Eustacia agrees to marry him, Clym watches her depart into a magnificent early summer landscape. He is, however, oppressed by its "horizontality which too much reminded him of the arena of life; it gave him a sense of bare equality with, and no superiority to, a single living thing under the sun." But of course the survivals may lead one to just this sense of equality, and not superiority, to all life. Obviously Clym still has all the pride of intellect that may prevent him from any intuitive grasp of the archaic mind and its equal participation in the natural world. Yet his failing eyesight soon brings this "unambitious" man so close, microscopically close to the intimate small life of the heath that "huge flies, ignorant of larders and wire-netting, and quite in a savage state, buzzed about him without knowing that he was a man." He is happy, calm, and he sings, much to the dismay of Eustacia, who feels that a real man would rebel at this reduction in social circumstances. Presumably Clym too is experiencing at least some small touch of the "savage state," and in this frame of mind he is a long way from a Jobian outrage that the universe has not been arranged according to man's ethical standards.

The long paragraph describing the life of the butterflies, grasshoppers, flies, snakes, and rabbits that constitute Clym's field of vision is one of the most contented passages Hardy every wrote, containing none of the outrage he ordinarily felt as man's dubious nativity. But it has taken a dire injury to get Clym to this point, and the plot-ridden section of the novel is just beginning. In it, Clym is so exhausted by tragedy and reduced by sheer chance and happenstance that it is almost as though Hardy were defending himself against a clear confrontation with the issues that crystallize immediately before all this pseudo-Greek claptrap begins.

Neither Clym nor Eustacia make very good tragic figures: Clym partly because so much of his energy is spent brooding over the death of a mother whose true nature is barely glimpsed in the falling out with her son over Eustacia. More important, however, is the reader's feeling that any tragedy appropriate to Clym must have a great deal to do with this approach to that strange, archaic otium that has been evolving throughout both *Far from the Madding Crowd* and *The Return of the Native*. In a very striking sense, Clym's alleged tragedy is nearly irrelevant to the true focus of the first two-thirds of the novel. Given the fundamental opposition of Clym and Eustacia, it might have been interesting to write a tragedy that would have told us more about the essential ontologies holding them apart. Instead the tragedy merely reiterates their incompatibility and leaves us with a "tragic" heroine whose main disappointment is that the only passionate opportunity on the horizon is breaking her marriage vows for a man, Wildeve, who "is not great enough" and "does not suffice for my desire!": "If he had been a Saul or a Bonaparte—ah! But to break my marriage vow for him—it is too poor a luxury!" There must be a difference between petulance, however impassioned, and tragic grief.

The potential tragedy of *The Return of the Native* lies in the native's not being able to return, if we understand *native* and *return* in the broadly evolutionary context I have established. Hardy will not explore the question of whether Clym, thoroughly disillusioned by the aspiring world and the new science, can return to a nature newly pregnant with a hitherto inconceivable antiquity and, abandoning the ego that makes him impose human ethics on nature, reach some consonance that is not dehumanizing. We are simply told by Hardy that following his assorted tragedies, Clym on the contrary will not "construct a hypothesis that shall . . . degrade a First Cause" and like most men will not "conceive a dominant power of lower moral quality than their own." He is no Job (who must be one of the "sternest of men") but comes remarkably close to being a meliorist. The great irony is that although in these days he feels closest to the ancient Celtic inhabitants of the heath, and "could almost live among them, look in their faces, and see them standing beside the barrows," it is Thomasin and not he who can respond to the maypole that spring, and to its "symbolic customs" and "Teutonic rites." Hardy lovingly describes its phallic adornment with flowers and reminds us that "Thomasin noticed all these, and was delighted that the May-revel was to be so near." Clym, though he later preaches from the Rainbarrow and no doubt still feels himself close to its ancient builders, has in some way slipped out of the archaic channels he had begun to enter.

Hardy takes care to indicate two entirely different kinds of involvement with the heath in these last pages. On one hand Hardy cannot think of Eustacia's intensifying antipathy to the heath without allowing his own grotesque imagination to run to extremes: "Skirting the pool she followed the path towards Rainbarrow, occasionally stumbling over twisted furze-roots, tufts of rushes, or oozing lumps of fleshy fungi, which at this season lay scattered about the heath like the rotten liver and lungs of some colossal animal. . . . She sighed bitterly and ceased to stand erect, gradually crouching down under the umbrella as if she were drawn into the barrow by a hand from beneath." These bizarre animations of the heath and barrow are half Hardy's and half Eustacia's, and they by no means suggest the consciousness of someone who has begun to enter the true spirit of the natural world by means of the survivals. Yet he certainly means to contrast them with Thomasin's difficult trip across the heath with her baby:

> Yet in spite of all this Thomasin was not sorry that she had started. To her there were not, as to Eustacia, demons in the air, and malice in every bush and bough. The drops which lashed her face were not scorpions, but prosy rain; Egdon in the mass was no monster whatever, but impersonal open ground. Her fears of the place were rational, her dislikes of its worst moods reasonable. At this time it was in her view a windy, wet place, in which a person might experience much discomfort, lose the path without care, and possibly catch cold.

Coming at such length and shortly before the impassioned death of Eustacia, Wildeve, and nearly of Clym, as well as before her marriage to the ultimate pragmatic idealist of them all (a man who can describe the "symbolic" maypole as "a lot of folk going crazy round a stick"), Thomasin's rationality is an important clue to Hardy's thinking at the end of this novel. Survival goes to Thomasin and Venn, somewhat as it does to Cathy and Hareton in *Wuthering Heights*. In this sense, they are really more nearly like the heath (with its genius for survival) than Clym, who although its true child has, like Ruskin, refused to accept survival as either Nature's or his own goal. Venn is an idealist too, loyal and even romantic beyond reason; yet he can both describe the maypole ritual as I have noted above and arrange for it to be staged just beyond Thomasin's front yard, knowing that she will respond to its ancient call as surely as Clym will not.

Yet of course Thomasin and Diggory Venn are no ideal for Hardy. These ruminations on the survival quality of a rational approach to the natural world serve to remind Hardy that, like the anthropologists themselves, Clym has found the "return" plagued with distortions born of his particularly advanced consciousness. Thomasin and Venn are not conscious as he is (albeit that most readers fault Hardy for not properly deepening this "continental" aspect of Clym's disillusionment). And, far more important, Thomasin and Venn do not really make the attempt, have never quite been native in the sense that Clym has. They have no way of knowing that even though Nature will not tolerate the imposition of peculiarly human prejudices—romantic, ethical, mechanistic, and so on—it offers survival (and a lesser contentment) to those who observe that a pragmatic approach to her mysteries is, ordinarily and at least, a safe one.

The end of *The Return of the Native* is as mysterious as the terms of its major problem suggest: the natural world (which of course must *include* man and especially his apparently aberrrant self-consciousness) is not rational, even though Thomasin's approach is best for survival. (Her approach is not foolproof, however, for on that night both she and her baby would have drowned had they not met Venn, with his characteristically detailed knowledge.) If Nature is not rationally arranged, at the end of the novel we are far from understanding what mentality a man might need to find himself consonant and at peace with it. This much the novel establishes quite vividly: any such ultimate peace, such ultimate return, need not be a dehumanizing experience. We are not led to believe either that Clym's near absorption by the heath (when his eyesight has failed and he turns furze-cutter) is the true return or that we should share Eustacia's and his mother's shock at what they see as a great social failure. Indeed, we cannot even feel that Clym has become nearly unconscious, although working till numb and sleeping like the dead. All we can say or need to at this point is that we apparently have a new and terribly elusive otium in the offing, a "peace" thoroughly influenced by the striking attempt of anthropologists from at least 1851 on to use the survival as the key to this kingdom.

That contentment and peace are what is sought we have affirmed by the continual testimony of Clym himself and by Hardy's refusal to undercut that goal in any significant way. What is so entirely remarkable about this novel is that Hardy does not immediately begin to erode Clym's conception of a return. He treats almost sarcastically Clym's theories of education, especially the idea that he can lead the natives from "the bucolic to the intellectual life" without offering them the intermediate stage of social advancement. Yet he never intimates that the ancient pastoral ideal has been invalidated by whatever modern virus has infected Clym. And this from a man so steeped in Darwin and the evolutionary anthropologists that we might expect him to conclude simply that a nature "red in fang and claw" could offer, to one seeking consonance with it, only savagery.

The status of the allegedly tragic action in *The Return of the Native* is the best clue we have to the continuing influence of the drive toward a pastoral return in this novel. Such action begins with a flurry immediately after Clym has drawn microscopically close the heath in that famous furze-cutting scene. He feels that the very presence of the heath (with its stoical endurance and characteristically untragic qualities) is antithetical to the passionate, incipiently tragic feelings he experiences while setting out on one of the distraught walks that will eventually bring him to his allegedly tragic identity as a kind of Oedipus. We may speculate that all this action toward a tragic identity for Clym is offered—within the phenomenological economy of both Hardy himself and the novel—as a kind of alternative to the pastoral identity which Clym has taken to such an extremity in the furze-cutting scene. There is every reason to believe that Hardy has offered the intense, tragic action as a surge of human dignity, of intense, egoistic identity; it is offered almost as an antidote to the potentially intimidating possibility of Clym's absorption by the heath in a scene where even the savage heath flies take him to be only another natural element. We do not need a long memory to recognize in Clym's approach to the very essence of the heath something from those earlier blurrings and white-outs and implosions so important to *Far from the Madding Crowd,* even if so small a thing as the song he sings maintains the crucial distance from Nature also signaled by Oak's flute on Norcombe Hill.

An explanation along these lines might then go on to claim that Clym attains his true identity—if not, by any stretch of the imagination, his fulfillment—precisely as a tragic and not a pastoral figure. In a very uncomfortable sense, the whole novel vibrates with the tensions between these tragic and pastoral identities. It is not my purpose here to claim that the pastoral thrust of even a frustrated and ambiguous deep return is the only authentic pulse of this novel, and that all the tragic denouement which is its avowed focus fails either to convince us or to allow Clym a significant stature at the end. On the contrary, the very presence of this basic tension between the pastoral and the tragic is in itself the most eloquent testimony imaginable that we are to take with the utmost seriousness the pastoral implications of the title. If the potency I have alleged in the possibility of a return is not there (if I have misread that pastoral aspect of the novel), why does Hardy even need to risk the embarrassment of relating Clym to

Oedipus and Christ? The tragic equipment of this novel, however the reader may feel about it, seems to have been an aesthetic necessity in order for Hardy to allow himself as much of the potent and even frightening new pastoral as he did. Having come really close to the strange new humility evoked by this at once newest and oldest heath-nature, Hardy must immediately have Clym straighten up, walk passionately here and there to gather the bits and pieces of information and experience he needs for an apparently unpastoral tragic identity and dignity. Hardy has not affirmed the tragic mode any more than he has rejected or undercut the pastoral. It may be that *The Return of the Native* in its most unique aesthetic purpose makes them a tribute to one another or has created, after the manner of *Far from the Madding Crowd,* another of those intense Hardian pairs, in which we may see how pastoral and tragedy depend on one another in the character of this Janus-like hero.

Chronology

1840	Thomas Hardy is born on June 2 in Higher Bockhampton, a community in the parish of Stinsford, Dorset; he is the son of Thomas Hardy, a stone mason, and Jemima Hand Hardy.
1848	Begins his education at a school in Lower Bockhampton.
1849	Is moved to a school in Dorchester.
1855	Begins teaching at the Stinsford Church Sunday School.
1856	Accepted at the office of architect John Hicks as pupil. Also in this year Hardy meets Horace Moule and William Barnes.
ca. 1860	Writes his first poem, "Domicilium."
1862	After settling in London, he goes to work for architect and church restorer Arthur Blomfield. He reads widely, studies paintings at the National Gallery, and becomes an agnostic.
1863	The Royal Institute of British Architects awards him an essay prize.
1865	*Chambers' Journal* publishes "How I Built Myself a House." Hardy attends French classes at King's College, Cambridge.
1867	Returns to Dorset and resumes working for John Hicks. Begins work on his first novel, *The Poor Man and the Lady*.
1868	*The Poor Man and the Lady* rejected by Macmillan; Hardy resubmits the manuscript to Chapman & Hall.
1869	Meets George Meredith. Begins his second novel, *Desperate Remedies*.
1870	Travels to Cornwall, where he meets Emma Lavinia Gifford, his future wife. Publisher William Tinsley agrees to produce *Desperate Remedies* at the author's expense.
1871	*Desperate Remedies* published. Also in this year Hardy writes *Under the Greenwood Tree* and begins *A Pair of Blue Eyes*.
1872	*Under the Greenwood Tree* published. *A Pair of Blue Eyes* appears in serial form.

1873 Hardy's friend Horace Moule commits suicide. Hardy is invited by Leslie Stephen to contribute to *Cornhill;* then he begins the serialized version of *Far from the Madding Crowd. A Pair of Blue Eyes* published.

1874 *Far from the Madding Crowd* published. Hardy marries Emma Lavinia Gifford; they travel to France after the wedding, and upon return settle in Surbiton.

1876 *The Hand of Ethelberta* appears. He and his wife travel to Holland and Germany, then move to a home at Sturminster Newton, in Dorset.

1878 *The Return of the Native* published. Hardy moves to London where he is elected to the Savile Club.

1880 *The Trumpet-Major* published. Hardy meets the Poet Laureate, Alfred, Lord Tennyson. The writing of *A Laodicean* is slowed by a serious illness.

1881 *A Laodicean* published.

1882 *Two on a Tower* published.

1883 Moves to Dorchester where he begins building his home, Max Gate. "The Dorsetshire Labourer" appears in *Longman's Magazine.*

1884 Begins composition of *The Mayor of Casterbridge.*

1885 Moves into Max Gate. Starts writing *The Woodlanders.*

1886 *The Mayor of Casterbridge* published.

1887 *The Woodlanders* published. Hardy visits Italy.

1888 *The Wessex Tales,* a collection of short stories, published. Composition of *Tess of the D'Urbervilles* begins.

1889 Several publishers reject the first installments of *Tess.*

1891 Both *Tess of the D'Urbervilles* and *A Group of Noble Dames* are published.

1892 Hardy's father dies. The first version of *The Well-Beloved* is serialized. Relations with his wife begin to deteriorate, and worsen over the next two years, particularly during the composition of *Jude the Obscure.*

1893 Travels to Dublin and Oxford, where he visits Florence Henniker, with whom he writes a short story, and, it is believed, falls in love.

1894 *Life's Little Ironies,* a collection of poems, published.

1895 *Jude the Obscure* is published and receives primarily outraged reviews. As a result Hardy decides to discontinue novel-writing and henceforward produces only poetry. Also in this year Hardy works on the Uniform Edition of his novels.

1897 *The Well-Beloved* published.
1898 Publishes *The Wessex Poems.*
1901 Publishes *Poems of the Past and the Present.*
1904 *The Dynasts,* part 1, published. Hardy's mother dies.
1905 Hardy receives an honorary LL.D. from Aberdeen.
1906 *The Dynasts,* part 2, published.
1908 *The Dynasts,* part 3, published.
1909 Publishes *Time's Laughingstocks.* Becomes the governor of the Dorchester Grammar School.
1910 Awarded the O.M. (Order of Merit).
1912 Hardy's wife Emma Lavinia dies on November 27.
1913 *A Changed Man* published. Hardy receives an honorary Litt.D. degree from Cambridge; he is also made an honorary Fellow of Magdalen College, Cambridge.
1914 Marries Florence Emily Dugdale. The collection of poems called *Satires of Circumstance* is published. As World War I begins Hardy joins a group of writers dedicated to the support of the Allied cause.
1915 Hardy's sister Mary dies.
1917 *Moments of Vision,* a collection of poetry, published.
1919 First *Collected Poems* published.
1920 Oxford University awards Hardy an honorary Litt.D.
1921 Publishes *Late Lyrics and Earlier.* Becomes honorary Fellow at Queen's College, Oxford.
1923 *The Famous Tragedy of the Queen of Cornwall* published. Receives a visit from the Prince of Wales at Max Gate.
1925 *Human Shows* published.
1928 Hardy dies on January 11; his ashes are buried at Westminster Abbey and his heart is placed at his first wife's grave in the Stinsford churchyard. *Winter Words* published posthumously. Florence Emily Hardy publishes *The Early Life of Thomas Hardy,* believed to have been written largely by Hardy himself.
1930 *Collected Poems* published posthumously. Florence Emily Hardy publishes *The Later Years of Thomas Hardy.*

Contributors

HAROLD BLOOM, Sterling Professor of the Humanities at Yale University, is the author of *The Anxiety of Influence, Poetry and Repression,* and many other volumes of literary criticism. His forthcoming study, *Freud: Transference and Authority,* attempts a full-scale reading of all of Freud's major writings. A MacArthur Prize Fellow, he is general editor of five series of literary criticism published by Chelsea House. During 1987–88, he was appointed Charles Eliot Norton Professor of Poetry at Harvard University.

D. H. LAWRENCE, major novelist, poet, and critic, is the author of such works as *Sons and Lovers, The Rainbow,* and *Women in Love.* His *Studies in Classic American Literature* remains one of the single most illuminating books on the American literary imagination.

IRVING HOWE is Distinguished Professor of English at Hunter College. His best-known book is *World of Our Fathers.* He is also known for his studies of Faulkner, Hardy, and Sherwood Anderson.

JEAN R. BROOKS is the author of *Thomas Hardy: The Poetic Structure.*

DAVID EGGENSCHWILER is Professor of English at the University of Southern California, Los Angeles, and the author of *The Christian Humanism of Flannery O'Connor.*

PERRY MEISEL is Associate Professor of English at New York University and the author of *Thomas Hardy: The Return of the Repressed.*

IAN GREGOR is Professor of Modern English Literature at the University of Kent. He is the author of several books and has edited a collection of critical essays on the Brontës.

AVROM FLEISHMAN is Professor of English at The Johns Hopkins University.

His books include *Fiction and the Ways of Knowing: Essays on British Novels, The English Historical Novel,* and *Figures of Autobiography.*

BRUCE JOHNSON is Professor of English at the University of Rochester and the author of *True Correspondence: A Phenomenology of Thomas Hardy's Novels* and *Conrad's Models of Mind.*

Bibliography

Abercrombie, Lascelles. *Thomas Hardy: A Critical Study*. London: Martin Secker, 1912.

Atkinson, F. G. " 'The Inevitable Movement Onward'—Some Aspects of *The Return of the Native*." *The Thomas Hardy Yearbook* 3 (1972): 10–17.

Bayley, John. *An Essay on Hardy*. Cambridge: Cambridge University Press, 1978.

Beach, Joseph Warren. *The Technique of Thomas Hardy*. Chicago: University of Chicago Press, 1922.

Beatty, C. J. P. "Two Noble Families in Thomas Hardy's *The Return of the Native*." *Notes and Queries* n.s. 23, vol. 221 (1976): 402–3.

Benvuto, Richard. "*The Return of the Native* as a Tragedy in Six Books." *Nineteenth-Century Fiction* 26 (1971): 83–93.

Bjork, Lennart. "Thomas Hardy's 'Hellenism.' " In *Papers on Language and Literature: Presented to Alvar Ellegard and Erik Frykman,* edited by Sven Backman and Goran Kjellmer, 46–58. Göteborg, Sweden: ACTA University Gothoburgensis, 1985.

———."Visible Essences as Thematic Structure in Hardy's *The Return of the Native*." *English Studies* 53 (1972): 52–63.

Bloom, Harold, ed. *Modern Critical Views: Thomas Hardy*. New Haven: Chelsea House, 1986.

Blunden, Edmund. *Thomas Hardy*. London: Macmillan, 1942.

Boumelha, Penny. *Thomas Hardy and Women: Sexual Ideology and Narrative Form*. Brighton, England: Harvester, 1982.

Brinkley, Richard. *Thomas Hardy as a Regional Novelist, with Special Reference to* The Return of the Native. St. Peter Port, Guernsey: Toucan, 1968.

Brooks, Jean R. *Thomas Hardy: The Poetic Structure*. Ithaca: Cornell University Press, 1971.

Brown, Douglas. *Thomas Hardy*. 1954. Reprint. Westport, Conn.: Greenwood, 1980.

Bullen, J. B. *The Expressive Eye: Fiction and Perception in the Work of Thomas Hardy*. Oxford: Clarendon, 1986.

Butler, Lance St. John. *Thomas Hardy*. British Authors Introductory Critical Studies. Cambridge: Cambridge University Press, 1978.

Carpenter, Richard. *Thomas Hardy*. New York: Twayne, 1964.

Casagrande, Peter J. *Unity in Hardy's Novels*. Lawrence: Regents Press of Kansas, 1982.

Cecil, David. *Hardy the Novelist*. New York: Bobbs-Merrill, 1946.

Chew, Samuel C. *Thomas Hardy: Poet and Novelist.* 2d ed. New York: Russell & Russell, 1964.
Cohen, Sandy. "Blind Clym, Unchristian Christian, and the Redness of the Reddleman: Character Correspondences in Hardy's *Return of the Native.*" *The Thomas Hardy Yearbook* 11 (1984): 49–55.
Corballis, Richard. "A Note on Mumming in *The Return of the Native.*" *The Thomas Hardy Yearbook* 5 (1976): 55–56.(Reprinted in *Notes and Queries* n.s. 25, vol. 223 [1978]: 323.)
Cornwall-Robinson, Margery. "Of Cows and Catfish: The Reading of Nature by Thomas Hardy and Loren Eiseley." *Soundings* 68 (1985): 52–61.
Crompton, Louis. "The Sunburnt God: Ritual and Tragic Myth in *The Return of the Native.*" *Boston University Studies in English* 4 (1960) 229–40.
Elliott, Albert Pettigrew. *Fatalism in the Works of Thomas Hardy.* Philadelphia: University of Pennsylvania Press, 1935.
Evans, Robert. "The Other Eustacia." *Novel* 1 (1968) 251–59.
Firor, Ruth A. *Folkways in Thomas Hardy.* Philadelphia: University of Pennsylvania Press, 1931.
Fleissner, Robert F. "A Return to Hardy's Native." *College English Association Critic* 28, no. 9 (1966): 7–8.
Gindin, James. "Critical Essays." In *Thomas Hardy:* The Return of the Native: *An Authoritative Text, Background, Criticism,* edited by James Gindin, 413–15. New York: Norton, 1969.
———."Hardy and Folklore." In *Thomas Hardy:* The Return of the Native: *An Authoritative Text, Background, Criticism,* edited by James Gindin, 396–401. New York: Norton, 1969.
———."Thomas Hardy." In *Harvest of a Quiet Eye: The Novel of Compassion,* 78–101. Bloomington: Indiana University Press, 1971.
Giordano, Frank R., Jr. "Eustacia Vye's Suicide." *Texas Studies in Literature and Language* 22 (1980): 504–21.
Gose, Elliott B., Jr. "*The Return of the Native.*" In *Imagination Indulged: The Irrational in the Nineteenth-Century Novel,* 95–125. Montreal: McGill-Queens University Press, 1972.
Gregor, Ian. *The Great Web: The Form of Hardy's Major Fiction.* London: Faber & Faber, 1974.
———."What Kind of Fiction Did Hardy Write?" *Essays in Criticism* 16 (1966): 290–308.
Guerard, Albert J. Introduction to *The Return of the Native,* by Thomas Hardy. New York: Holt, Rinehart & Winston, 1969.
———, ed. *Hardy: A Collection of Critical Essays.* Englewood Cliffs, N. J.: Prentice-Hall, 1963.
Hinz, Evelyn. "Hierogamy versus Wedlock: Types of Marriage Plots and Their Relationship to Genres of Prose Fiction." *PMLA* 91 (1976): 900–13.
Hornback, Bert A. *The Metaphor of Chance: Vision and Technique in the Works of Thomas Hardy.* Athens: Ohio University Press, 1971.
Howe, Irving. *Thomas Hardy.* New York: Macmillan, 1967.
Huss, Roy. "Social Change and Moral Decay in the Novels of Thomas Hardy." *Dalhousie Review* 47 (1967): 28–44.

Janett, David W. "Eustacia Vye and Eula Varner, Olympians: The Worlds of Thomas Hardy and William Faulkner." *Novel* 6 (1973): 163–74.
Johnson, Bruce. *True Correspondence: A Phenomenology of Thomas Hardy's Novels.* Tallahassee: University Presses of Florida, 1983.
Kennard, Jean E. *Victims of Convention.* Hamden, Conn.: Archon, 1978.
Kramer, Dale. *Thomas Hardy: The Forms of Tragedy.* Detroit: Wayne State University Press, 1975.
———."Unity of Time in *The Return of the Native.*" *Notes and Queries* n.s. 12, vol. 210 (1965): 3043–45.
Liao, Tianliang. "The Root Cause of the Tragedy in *The Return of the Native.*" *Foreign Literature Studies* (China) 29, no. 3 (1985): 140–42.
Litz, A. Walton. Introduction to *The Return of the Native,* by Thomas Hardy. New York: Houghton Mifflin, 1967.
Lodge, David. "Thomas Hardy as a Cinematic Novelist." In *Thomas Hardy after Fifty Years,* edited by Lance St. John Butler, 78–79. Totowa, N.J.: Rowman & Littlefield, 1977.
McKenna, John. "Clym Yeobright's Eleventh Commandment." *American Notes and Queries* 17 (1978): 8–9.
Marshal, George O., Jr. "Thomas Hardy's Eye Imagery." *Colby Library Quarterly* 7 (1966): 264–68.
Martin, Bruce K. "Whatever Happened to Eustacia Vye?" *Studies in the Novel* 4 (1972): 619–27. Special Thomas Hardy Issue
May, Derwent. Introduction to *The Return of the Native,* by Thomas Hardy. London: Macmillan, 1975.
Meisel, Perry. *Thomas Hardy: The Return of the Repressed.* New Haven: Yale University Press, 1971.
Mickelson, Anne Z. "The Family Trap in *The Return of the Native.*" *Colby Library Quarterly* 10 (1974): 463–75.
Miller, J. Hillis. *Thomas Hardy: Distance and Desire.* Cambridge: Harvard University Press, 1970.
Millgate, Michael. *Thomas Hardy: His Career as a Novelist.* New York: Random House, 1971.
———."Thomas Hardy's *The Return of the Native.*" *Venture* 6 (1970): 3–17.
Morrell, Roy. *Thomas Hardy: The Will and the Way.* Singapore: University of Malaysia Press, 1965.
Osborne, L. MacKenzie. "The Chronological Frontier in Thomas Hardy's Novels." *Studies in the Novel* 4 (1972): 543–55. Special Thomas Hardy Issue
Paterson, John. Introduction to *The Return of the Native,* by Thomas Hardy. New York: Harper & Row, 1966.
———. *The Making of* The Return of the Native. Berkeley: University of California Press, 1960.
———. "*The Return of the Native* as Antichristian Document." Nineteenth-Century Fiction 14 (1959) 111–27.
Peck, John. "Hardy's Novel Endings." *Journal of the Eighteen Nineties Society* 9 (1978): 10–15.
Pinion, F. B. *A Hardy Companion: A Guide to the Works of Thomas Hardy and Their Background.* New York: St. Martin's, 1968.

———. "The Ranging Vision." In *Thomas Hardy after Fifty Years,* edited by Lance St. John Butler, 1–12. Totowa, N.J.: Rowman & Littlefield, 1977.

Sankey, Benjamin. "Hardy's Plotting." *Twentieth Century Literature* 11 (1965): 82–97.

Sasaki, Hisako. "The Twofold Function of Time and Space in *The Return of the Native.*" *Bulletin of the Thomas Hardy Society of Japan, A Special Issue* (1978): 57–67.

Schwarz, Daniel R. "The Narrator as Character in Hardy's Major Fiction." *Modern Fiction Studies* 18 (1972): 155–72.

Sherman, G. W. *The Pessimism of Thomas Hardy*. Rutherford, N.J.: Fairleigh Dickinson University Press, 1976.

Southerington, F. R. "*The Return of the Native:* Thomas Hardy and the Evolution of Consciousness." In *Thomas Hardy and the Modern World,* edited by F. B. Pinion, 37–47. Dorchester, England: The Thomas Hardy Society, 1974.

Starzyk, Lawrence J. "The Coming Universal Wish Not to Live in Hardy's 'Modern' Novels." *Nineteenth-Century Fiction* 26 (1972): 419–35.

Stewart, J. I. M. *Thomas Hardy: A Critical Biography*. New York: Dodd, Mead, 1971.

Swets, Marinus M. "Understanding Hardy's *The Return of the Native* through His Poetry." *Exercise Exchange* 12 (1965): 4–6.

Temblett-Wood, J. C. S. Introduction to *The Return of the Native,* by Thomas Hardy. London: Macmillan, 1975.

Thomas Hardy Annual, 1983–.

The Thomas Hardy Society Review, 1975–.

The Thomas Hardy Yearbook, 1970–.

Thurley, Geoffrey. *The Psychology of Hardy's Novels*. Queensland: University of Queensland Press, 1975.

Toliver, Harold E. "Hardy's Novels of Scene and Manners." In *Pastoral Forms and Attitudes,* 274–300. Berkeley and Los Angeles: University of California Press, 1971.

Vigar, Penelope. *The Novels of Thomas Hardy: Illusion and Reality*. London: Athlone, 1974.

Wyatt, Bryant N. "Poetic Justice in *The Return of the Native.*" *Mark Twain Journal* 21, no. 4 (1983): 56–57.

Yoshikawa, Michio. "An Aspect of Hardy's Style: The Description of Egdon Heath." *Bulletin of the Thomas Hardy Society of Japan, A Special Issue* (1978): 49–56.

Zellefrow, Ken. "*The Return of the Native:* Hardy's Map and Eustacia's Suicide." *Nineteenth-Century Fiction* 28 (1973): 214–20.

Acknowledgments

"From 'Study of Thomas Hardy': *The Return of the Native*" (originally entitled "Containing Six Novels and the Real Tragedy") by D. H. Lawrence from *Phoenix: The Posthumous Papers of D. H. Lawrence*, edited by Edward D. McDonald, © 1936 by Frieda Lawrence, © renewed 1964 by the Estate of Frieda Lawrence Ravagli. Reprinted by permission of Viking Penguin, Inc. and Laurence Pollinger Ltd.

"*The Return of the Native*" (originally entitled "The World of the Wessex") by Irving Howe from *Thomas Hardy* by Irving Howe, © 1966, 1967, 1985 by Irving Howe. Reprinted by permission of Macmillan Publishing Company and Macmillan Press Ltd., London and Basingstoke.

"*The Return of the Native:* A Novel of Environment" by Jean R. Brooks from *Thomas Hardy: The Poetic Structure* by Jean R. Brooks, © 1971 by Jean R. Brooks. Reprinted by permission of Elek Books Ltd., a division of Grafton Books.

"Eustacia Vye, Queen of Night and Courtly Pretender" by David Eggenschwiler from *Nineteenth-Century Fiction* 25, no. 4 (March 1971), © 1971 by the Regents of the University of California. Reprinted by permission of the University of California Press.

"The Return of the Repressed" (originally entitled "*The Return of the Native*") by Perry Meisel from *Thomas Hardy: The Return of the Repressed: A Study of the Major Fiction* by Perry Meisel, © 1972 by Yale University. Reprinted by permission of Yale University Press.

"Landscape with Figures" (originally entitled "Chapter 1") by Ian Gregor from *The Great Web: The Form of Hardy's Major Fiction* by Ian Gregor, © 1974 by Ian Gregor. Reprinted by permission of Faber and Faber Ltd.

"The Buried Giant of Egdon Heath" by Avrom Fleishman from *Fiction and the Ways of Knowing: Essays on British Novels* by Avrom Fleishman, © 1978 by the University of Texas Press. Reprinted by permission of the author and the University of Texas Press, publisher.

"Pastoralism and Modernity" (originally entitled *"The Return of the Native"*) by Bruce Johnson from *True Correspondence: A Phenomenology of Thomas Hardy's Novels* by Bruce Johnson, © 1983 by the Board of Regents of the State of Florida. Reprinted by permission.

Index